"Bring the power of God's Love more fully into your daily life."

Prophet Del Hall

Welcome to Book One of our *Zoom With Prophet* series. It is a transcript of the January 2, 2021 Zoom With Prophet meeting titled *Your Magnificent Eternal Self*.

It also includes some comments from YouTube viewers as well as ten additional testimonies from Prophet's disciples. These will add clarity to the Zoom meeting topic of this book.

Cover: The drop of water on the cover was inspired by the beauty of the real you, Soul, your magnificent eternal self, cradled lovingly on a feather. Soul is a thing of true beauty that exists because God loves It.

YOUR MAGNIFICENT ETERNAL SELF

Editor: Lorraine Fortier

Assistant Editors: Lynne Hall, Del Hall IV, Cathy Sandman

Cover Image by Ledyx/shutterstock.com

Cover Design by Del Hall IV

No part of this publication may be reproduced, stored in or introduced into a retrieval system, or transmitted, in any form or by any means (electronically, mechanical, photocopying, recording or otherwise), without the prior written permission of both the copyright owner and the publisher of this book. Re-selling through electronic outlets (like Amazon, Barnes and Noble or eBay) without permission of the publisher is illegal and punishable by law. The scanning, uploading, and distribution of this book via the Internet or via any other means without the permission of the publisher is illegal and punishable by law. Please purchase only authorized editions and do not participate in or encourage electronic piracy of copyrightable materials. Your support of the author's right is appreciated.

Copyright © 2022 F.U.N. Inc. All rights reserved.

ISBN: 978-1-947255-09-8

YOUR MAGNIFICENT ETERNAL SELF

PROPHET DEL HALL

"The days of any religion or path coming between me and my children are coming to an end," saith the Lord

DECEMBER 29, 2013

TABLE OF CONTENTS

Part One: "Your Magnificent Eternal Self" Transcript 1

Part Two: YouTube Audience Comments .. 53

Part Three: Disciple Testimonies 65

    Precious and Beautiful in God's Eyes 67

    My First Glimpse of Soul 73

    Child of God — Really 76

    I Am Light and Sound 79

    Truth Uncovered 84

    Captain's Chair 89

    Through the Eyes of Soul 95

    I Held Her in Heaven 100

    A Child of God is Born 105

    I Am Soul 109

Part Four: What It Is Like Living from a Higher View of Life 117

Appendix
Guidance for a Better Life Our Story 129
    My Father's Journey 129
    My Son, Del Hall IV 139
What is the Role of God's Prophet? 143
HU — An Ancient Name For God 151
Articles of Faith 153
Contact Information 163
Additional Reading 165

Part One: "Your Magnificent Eternal Self" Transcript

Today welcome to *Zoom With Prophet*. Today's topic I think is, I hope is, going to be interesting; it's your "Magnificent Eternal Self," and we call that Soul, but I thought magnificent eternal self was a better description than just the word Soul. What I'm hoping to do today for those that operate more as Soul, as most of my disciples do, I am hoping maybe you will hear something a little different than you have heard before or I'll remind you of something maybe over the years you have forgotten about. And for the newer folks that do not operate as Soul yet, I hope I motivate you to consider staying spiritually nourished too so you can operate more as Soul. I hope to make a case today that this is not just a kind of academic discussion, but when you operate as Soul and understand your eternal self, there are very, very significant advantages to building an abundant life. When you operate as Soul and understand your true eternal self, which is stunning, you are all stunning, and know how God sees you, this is not just an academic discussion. I am hoping to make a case because I believe it, that it really, really is a huge advantage in life to operate as Soul.

So let's get started. Your magnificent eternal self. I want to start out on a very practical level. One of the reasons, and this might be something my students know but maybe they haven't thought about, one of the reasons that my disciples up at Guidance for a Better Life retreat center have grown so, so much to a very, very high level spiritually — I believe their lives are in balance for the most part, and I believe they have abundant, basically happy, joyful lives is because they have not just grown physically. There are two parts of you; let's say you have this physical part, the part you see when you look in the mirror, the part I see when I look at you. You see your face, you brush your teeth, you comb your hair, but there's another part of you, your magnificent eternal self that we also grow; we do not just grow our physical selves. What if you grow your physical self, and you get really wise spiritually and then when you pass away, what does that wisdom do for you? It pretty much stays here and is probably buried or cremated. It does not do too much. This is not exact but it's pretty close. But when we grow both our physical self to have an abundant life and we also grow our eternal self that continues after we pass on, can you see that wisdom and growth and spiritual maturity that Heavenly Father wants us to have, it continues? Because as Soul, your eternal self, you continue. So I think one of the things I want to try to point out today is that if you really want to grow, and grow efficiently and effectively and in balance, we want to grow this part of us, the physical self here, this part I see when I look in a mirror, but we also want to grow our eternal self. And I hope I make a case today why that is such a gigantic advantage in life, both in this life and in the long-term view of your many lives down the road.

A lot of the experiences we have up at the retreat center we can only have as Soul. That is the other premise today. If we only had experiences in our physical body, I think most of my students know there would not be much to do. We could talk about stuff, we could read some beautiful scripture, but I think most of us learn best through experience. If you want to learn how to swing a baseball bat and hit a ball, you can talk about it, read about it all you want, but it's not the same as getting out and swinging a bat and trying to hit a ball. There is a difference. Can I get a thumbs-up on that? Thank you. We learn mostly through experience. So many of the things we do up at the retreat center we do as Soul. We spend a great deal, and this is for the newer folks, we spend a great deal of time developing, understanding, and experiencing our magnificent eternal self. And if you have not thought about it that is a gigantic advantage in growth, not only for this lifetime, but you maintain that wisdom and your connection with Prophet and the Heavenly Father when you grow as Soul. So, we'll move on here.

So what exactly is this eternal self? I've said it, it is Soul. It's easier to say Soul, and that is the term we use, easier than saying magnificent eternal self although I love that title. Now I have heard a lot of people since I was a kid talk about Soul, and I hear them say this phrase or something similar. They say "I have a Soul," and I think all my students know that no, "You are Soul." And I want to try to make a case for you, for the newer folks. When your physical bodies wear out, the thing you are continues on. If you say "I have a Soul" and you identify with your physical bodies and then you pass away, can you see the disconnect? You continue on, but the part that you identified with, your physical body, is no longer functional. Yet some paths say you continue on. If you say "I am Soul" that has a physical body, when the physical body wears out after eighty to one hundred years, then the thing you are and you identify with can continue on, and you go to the Heavens, different Heavens, then sometime in the future come back into a body. So when you start, and this takes a while, but once you realize you are Soul, your eternal self that is temporarily residing in a physical body, that I call an "Earth suit," you start to see that when your body wears out, the thing you are, not a thing you have, then goes on to the Heavens, one of the mansions in the Father's House, and you get a new body that looks very similar to you now. Then eventually you come back, maybe reincarnate. Once you identify that you are Soul first, and you have been around for a long, long time, that has a body occasionally, a lot of things like reincarnation and many other teachings all of a sudden make perfect sense. But if you say you "Have a Soul" there is always a bit of a disconnect that bothers me when people say that, and then they say they go on to Heaven. Well their body that they identify with cannot go on because it's going to stay here; I just feel sad for them. I hope to clear that up today. I think all my students identify that you are Soul forever that has a body temporarily, and I call it an "Earth suit."

So how long have you existed? We say your magnificent eternal self. I actually do not know, but I would say many thousands of years minimum. Probably much more? A very, very long long time. And over that long period of time you as Soul have gained a great deal of experience. You have had many opportunities as Soul to come temporarily into an "Earth suit," a physical body, and you have had many, many lifetimes. You have probably gone through every challenge imaginable in your life as Soul, not in this life, but as Soul, you probably have gone through every imaginable challenge and test you could possibly have over hundreds of incarnations. You also then, as Soul, get a body in the higher Heavens; so you may have many lifetimes in the higher Heavens where again you are getting experience. So I want to make a case today if you start operating more as Soul, which we'll talk about, think of the advantage it is in this life if you have multiple lifetimes of experience, and you can bring that into this life. Can you imagine how much more confidence you would have when you have a challenge at work, in relationships, raising kids, jobs, whatever? You have been through so many challenges and as you start operating as Soul, your eternal self, much of that wisdom now becomes available. Imagine having a hundred lifetimes to learn from: marriages, raising kids, jobs, health issues, all kinds of issues. If we just identify with the physical body we do not have that experience and that wisdom, but as we start operating as Soul, which I will talk about later, you are literally bringing in wisdom of your true eternal self, and you make better decisions: You know what is right for you, you know what type of life would make you the happiest, and on and on. So that is a huge advantage to start operating more as Soul because you have all that wealth of experience and wisdom to tap into.

The Christian view, let me start there. The Christian view, which is pretty close, says we were created in Heaven, and that is true; God created all of you out of His Love, and I will talk more about that, on the twelfth Heaven. He created you, not your physical body, but you as Soul, the real you. But the Christian view is because you were immature you only thought of yourself, that you were punished by sending you down here to learn to become more mature. But think about it. Do you think

God, the Heavenly Father, was surprised that when He first created you, you were immature and did not have a lot of experience? Imagine having a child that's six weeks old and they cannot write. It would not surprise you they cannot write, that they cannot control their bowel movements; they need a diaper. I do not think God was surprised that we were immature. So He did not punish us; it was a gift of love to bring us down, over lifetimes, to get a physical body, an "Earth suit," to reside in to learn some lessons to become more spiritually mature. So the Christian view is true. God created us in the Heavens, the twelfth Heaven which a lot of us have visited, but it was a gift of love, and God was not surprised we were immature; we were just born spiritually a long, long time ago. So of course it did not surprise Him. He sent us as Soul that He created in the Heavens and put us down here; over time, it was a transition, and put us in one of these physical bodies, but *this* [Prophet pointing to his physical body] is not the real eternal us. Our physical bodies are a gift to be treasured and taken care of, but the real us when God originally created us, He did not create our physical bodies, He created the eternal us, Soul. And He has given us many, many lifetimes in physical bodies. If you know you are Soul, then it makes sense; you could have many, many bodies and many, many experiences over thousands and thousands of years. So the main thing is when I hear Christians and other people talk about they were created by God in Heaven, I do not know if they really think about what they are saying. And maybe you all know, this may be kind of a waste of time, but I want to mention, I think they think the physical body is what was created; that they were created in their physical bodies. I do not know if they actually think about it, that God created them first as Soul at the twelfth Heaven. I think they look in the mirror and assume they were created in a body like *this* [Prophet pointing to his physical body]. No, they were created as a ball of God's Light and Love.

So what is Soul actually made out of? God created us out of His Essence. Another term for His Essence that we are familiar with is the Holy Spirit, but what is the Holy Spirit? We can be more specific with the definition of the Holy Spirit; we say it's made out of God's Light and His Sound, which most of you have experienced. So we are made out of a small, individualized piece of God's Holy Spirit, His Voice, His Essence. Another term for the Holy Spirit that I do not hear very often is God's Love. You are all incredible. You were made out of a small individualized piece of God's Love, His Holy Spirit, His Voice, His Essence but not this physical body. The physical body is a separate gift down here in this physical world. You were created out of the Voice of God.

I have heard people say only Jesus was divine, maybe some apostles or saints, but think about it, if you are literally a child of God and you are made out of His Voice, are you not divine also? Would you all give me a thumbs-up if you agree with me? Is God's Voice, the Holy Spirit, divine? Yes? So if you are made out of the Holy Spirit, a small individualized piece, not all of it, would you be therefore considered by definition divine and holy? Absolutely. And when I hear — thanks for the thumbs-up Bobby, hey good to see you Joan, "hi." I think that may be something second nature to you folks, but when I hear most people out there in the world saying so-and-so's divine, but they're not; it just makes me sad because when they look in the mirror all they see is their physical self. They only see the sheath; it's just the outer covering of this stunning ball of God's Love and Light, literally a piece of the Holy Spirit. So all of God's children whether they are doing things we like, whether we do not like them, whether they are doing things that are not very nice, they are all made from a beautiful piece of the Holy Spirit. They may not be doing very well with it, but everybody in town, even the people you do not like, even politicians we're really not happy with, they still deserve a certain amount of respect because they are also made with a piece of God's Voice. And when people say we are made in the image of God, I think most people think your physical body. God can take a shape like that if He chooses; He can take many forms. But which is more accurate, you are made in the image of God in your physical "Earth suits" or this beautiful ball of radiant glowing light? It is of course the latter. The image of God that we are made in is the image of the Holy Spirit. That is very accurate, and I think much more accurate and realistic than an image of a physical body like we are all looking at here.

So when this part that we have, which we do not have **we are**, when it leaves the physical body, when our body wears out after a certain period of time, once it leaves permanently our body is no longer functional. So the body, it is almost self-evident, is not the real us. The real eternal us, Soul, is the thing that is made in Heaven out of the Voice of God. Soul comes to the lower worlds, gets into an "Earth suit" (a body) because it's so refined and so beautiful this ball of light that it needs to place a shield-like something over it to protect it, so it comes into a physical body. When the body translates the real you, your magnificent eternal self, this beautiful, stunning, divine being, goes on to the other Heavens where God will give you a new body that looks very much the same. I hope for the newer folks you start to at least consider, and you might just consider it, you do not have to agree, that you truly are Soul that *has a body*, temporarily, but as Soul you go on forever and ever. And someday you will get a new physical body or an astral body or a causal body, but the real you is so much more stunning than these bodies. As beautiful as you all are as Soul, it's almost beyond concept until you see yourself how incredibly magnificent and beautiful you truly are. And you are all divine children of God.

Before we continue, I just want to review. What is Soul again? It is literally the Light and Sound of God; that is actually what Soul is made of and that is divine. You are all divine. So will that make you magnificent? You're magnificent to me in your physical bodies, but our physical bodies no matter how gorgeous and how smart cannot compare with the wisdom and the stunning beauty of your eternal self we call Soul. Just think about that for a moment. What if this is true for the newer folks, that the real you is a divine spark of the Holy Spirit? That's, that is really quite stunning. And I want to get beyond just how cool you are, I want to show you the advantages of actually operating more as Soul. It is a gigantic advantage in life to start bringing that part of you into daily life with all Its wisdom. Let me check my notes.

When you look into a mirror, how many of you see yourself as Soul when you look into a mirror? Do some of my students actually see that ball of light or do you just see you need to shave or brush your teeth or put on makeup? I'm actually curious about this; I had not thought about this. Do my disciples actually see that ball of light or is it only when we have special spiritual experiences up at the retreat center? Or do you mostly just see the sheath covering the ball of light? Any of you, thumbs-up, do you actually see the ball light? You do Terry? Okay. Most of the time even though I know I'm a ball of light as Soul, and we are all the same, we are all equal as Soul, Soul equals Soul, most of the time I just see this old face that needs a shave, that is getting age spots and the hair is getting thin. I do not every day see myself as Soul. I do not see the ball of light, if I did it would be hard to shave. Actually I'm glad; I probably would cut myself shaving, and my hair would be a real mess trying to comb a ball of light. But I know I am Soul that has this old body, and I think most of you do also. I am happy to see my physical self when I shave — shaving a ball of light, that could be very hazardous to your health, but thanks for playing Terry.

We are all made of this light, Soul equals Soul. All of God's children, the ones we like the ones we do not like, good people and bad people, all are divine sparks of the Holy Spirit. So if Soul equals Soul, when we were created that was our raw material, how come we are all so different? If we are created out of the same raw material and Soul equals Soul, we have read that in scripture, then why are we all so very beautifully unique? And God loves our uniqueness. Well, let's go back to having lived maybe hundreds of lives; your experiences when you are in a body in

Heaven, an astral body or causal body, are different than other people's experiences. When you incarnate once-in-a-while down here in a physical body, every one of our experiences every day is slightly different than everybody else's. Can we get a thumbs-up on that? So over time if you take the same raw material, these little baby Souls up in Heaven, these immature balls of light and sound, and send them down here to become more mature, all these experiences both when in the Heavens, the Father's mansions, for periods of time and when incarnated on Earth, all these experiences make each Soul unique, and God loves that, that is actually a positive. Every day we become a little more unique than somebody else and over thousands, maybe at least hundreds of incarnations both the ones above and below, we become our beautiful unique individualized self. So we are all an individualized piece of the Holy Spirit, God's Light and Sound, that means we are divine. And when we first came down here we were pretty much all the same, but after each incarnation we pick up certain likes, certain things we do not like so much, we have certain opinions, we're drawn to certain topics we are interested in, certain other things we are not so interested in. So God loves that these Souls individualized over time, He loves our uniqueness, and our uniqueness is so much more profound than what most people nowadays talk about: skin color uniqueness, male female, nationality. Those are unique but whether we are all the same skin color, all the same nationality, we are all male or female, the uniqueness of Soul is a much more interesting uniqueness. I hope you all see that. The social consciousness about uniqueness that you have to have different colors, different races that's fine, but frankly we are so much more unique than just skin color, background, country we come from, male or female, or whatever else. We are all extremely unique, and I do not think most people see that. And God, a lot of people think uniqueness is good, well God specializes in it. Every experience we have makes us extraordinarily unique, and God loves our uniqueness. So Soul does equal Soul; we are always the same raw material, all of us are always eternal, all Souls have an incredible potential, which I want to get into, that can bring more abundance in our life if we nurture Soul. So all of us have this stunning advantage if we wake up Soul, which we will get into in a moment, but we're also ... it is kind of the best of both worlds; we have the same raw material, the same potential which is stunning, your potential is stunning all of you, but we are also extremely unique. It is really a beautiful combination. So if you wonder if God's into uniqueness, He's probably ... He is the one that invented it. So I hope you embrace your uniqueness, it's a beautiful thing. Yet, we have this connection that brings us together; we are all Soul. We are all children of God made in His image out of a piece of the Holy Spirit, not so much in our physical bodies. It is a beautiful balance.

I want to get back to what I said early on. We spend a great deal of time up at the retreat center talking about Soul but also operating as Soul, nourishing Soul, and having experiences that most people on the planet have no clue are even possible, as Soul. So if we did not spend a lot of time understanding our eternal self, our magnificent eternal self, and learning to wake Soul up and operate as Soul and nourish It, most of the spiritual experiences we have at the retreat center we could not have. We could not go to God's Temples of Learning in Heaven. We could not go into Spirit and travel the Heavens. We could not go and meet the Heavenly Father. So let me talk about that a bit. How do we wake up Soul and get the tremendous advantage that Soul is, to wake It up and make It operational? We have this part of us over here, if you see my hand let me put my cards down. This is our physical self, and we can spend our whole life trying to become the best we can physically. Then over here we have our eternal self, which is the real us, Soul that goes on forever. What if we just try to be the best physically we can be and totally forget Soul? That would be a very lopsided, out of balance, and very inefficient way to grow in my view. So up at the retreat center, which I mentioned earlier, we try to grow as "two-leggeds" in our physical bodies; we try to become more balanced, more grateful, better people, able to give and receive love more, and on and on, just better people. But we also work as much, maybe more, on our eternal selves. Can you imagine the advantage in life if we have a group of people that grow both spiritually as their eternal self and their physical self? Can you imagine the advantage of growing both what I call your higher eternal self and our lower physical self? That is a gigantic advantage, which I'm going to have a whole bunch of things I hope to share with you. Most people grow only their physical self.

How do we grow and take the advantage of all the wisdom and experience gained, of all your lifetimes, of all your incarnations both here and your incarnations in the various Heavens? How do we take advantage of that incredible, incredible wisdom and experience? We have to wake up Soul. Soul is kind of awake, but much of It is dormant. We are alive, if it was not awake somewhat we would not, our body would not function. Soul is what animates our body and when Soul leaves the body permanently the body no longer is functional. But how do we get It to do more than just kind of survive and keep us breathing every day? We have to wake It up, and I will put that in quotes "wake It up." And we all know this but I would like to review, we need spiritual food. Jesus talked about in the Bible several times that you need your daily bread. And I have said this before in many of my videos, he was not talking about physical bread; he was talking about spiritual bread or spiritual nourishment. And a quick review if you do not eat physical food for your physical "Earth suit" over weeks and months you would perish. First you just get sleepy, you would become weak, you could not think very clearly, and eventually if you did not get some physical nourishment you would eventually perish. Well Soul, It functions okay, we can breathe and function but we do not get the benefits of the wisdom, the incredible wisdom and experience that Soul can bring us.

What is the other benefit that Soul is incredible at? If God guides us through His

Holy Spirit, then if we want to receive God's guidance do we need to tune in to the Holy Spirit? Yes, of course, that is how He guides us. So which would be better, our physical brains tuning in to the Holy Spirit, the Voice of God, or tuning in to Prophet which is a concentrated aspect of Holy Spirit, or would something, for example Soul, made out of the Holy Spirit be better at communicating with the Holy Spirit? It is almost intuitive that our brains can communicate and understand guidance, but our true eternal self is much better able to understand the guidance of the Heavenly Father because It is made of the same stuff, the same cloth, His Voice. How do we get that tremendous advantage in life of all that experience and knowledge and wisdom through all our incarnations? Plus, how do we ... if we want guidance from the Heavenly Father, if we wake up Soul we get so much better at understanding His guidance. So we must more fully wake up Soul, and how do we do that? We get our daily bread, our daily spiritual nourishment. And I think you all know singing HU is our cornerstone, our foundation, for spiritual nourishment. Singing "HUUUUUUUUUUU," that love song to God, it nourishes Soul. And what specifically nourishes Soul? The Light and Sound of God is the food for Soul. When you sing HU you become very receptive to the Light and Sound of God, the Holy Spirit. You may not perceive it for years. You may have to HU a long time before you are aware of it, but you become receptive and when you become receptive to the Holy Spirit, the Holy Spirit comes into you more fully and nourishes your eternal self, the real you, Soul. And when Soul gets daily spiritual nourishment by singing HU, one of the best ways, it starts kind of waking up and then that wisdom from lifetimes starts benefiting you. You just start knowing the right thing in life, the right people to hang with, the type of career, you just start knowing basically yourself better, and you start making decisions that work for you. Can you see that?

You literally start being introduced to you. As that eternal part of you wakes up you just know stuff. You have this knowingness what is right, what is best for you, what is in your heart, what are your dreams, because the real you is where those things reside, not so much in our physical bodies. And then if you want to develop a relationship with the Heavenly Father and listen to His guidance, and to feel His Love and His comfort and His joy, the part of you, the eternal you that is made out of His Essence, is very good at understanding His language. So we need to feed Soul daily: singing HU is one way; reading scripture can provide spiritual nourishment; being in the presence of God's Prophet, which is a concentrated aspect of the Holy Spirit, whether on the inner or physically, that's very nourishing. In my book *Spiritual Keys For a More Abundant Life*, for extreme spiritual nourishment, a very high level of nourishment is when you are in "Prophet's Inner Presence," and if you all have that book you might look at that Spiritual Key, and most of you are doing that now. So reading scripture, being in Prophet's presence, contemplating, praying, all these things, but singing HU I would think would be the cornerstone to receiving spiritual nourishment — spiritual food, for some of you that have been around awhile, being in the presence of Prophet in addition to singing HU. Those two give extreme amounts of spiritual nourishment, which is the Holy Spirit that feeds the little piece of the Holy Spirit that you are. Pretty good system the Heavenly Father created.

When you wake yourself up, you start truly knowing who you are and what your likes are, what your interests are, and for example, let's say some of you ... you know people that reenact the Civil War; they get into this stuff on weekends. It is very possible that they had a past life during the Civil War, and they are still drawn to that. Or maybe some are really into studying ancient Egypt. You may find out as you wake up Soul you start getting interested in ancient Egypt, that maybe you are being guided to study that history because maybe you had a past life in ancient Egypt, and so many things start making sense. So singing HU, and that is why I encourage I think at every retreat, I am always encouraging and pushing a little bit early on, you must get your daily spiritual bread. It is absolutely, it is absolutely a must to benefit from all this wisdom and experience of Soul, and the ability to know Divine guidance better than our intellect, and to know the real you, and also get a lot of healings and things from past lives; you have to get that daily spiritual bread. So Jesus and I are saying the same thing. And it is so wonderful that all of you pretty much, even the new folks, I know Michelle and a lot of the newer folks are HUing. That is how to receive your daily bread and that will give you such an advantage in life because you bring in your eternal self. And even if you are not interested in Divine guidance, and I know you all are, or a relationship with Heavenly Father, it is such an advantage to have the real self woken up. Can you all kind of ... I don't think I have ever explained it that way. Can you see the gigantic advantage of your eternal self with all that experience being woken up and guiding you in your daily life? Can you kind of see that? It's stunning.

I do not want this just to be a philosophical, churchy discussion. How many angels dance on the head of the pin, yeah, who cares? Depends how big the pin is, if it is a really big pin they all can dance. Nobody ever thinks of it that way, so that is definitely another way to look at it, but that is enough for today. But it is a huge practical advantage to living your life, and if you want to progress on your spiritual journey it's, it is almost a must, but either way receiving daily spiritual bread is a huge advantage. So what I want to do now, and I have got a note here, "additional benefits of operating as Soul." I am really trying to do a sales job today to keep you getting your daily spiritual bread, and if you do not do much else things will start falling into place. You will start being the person that you really want to be. Your life will fall into place. So first thing is you need to get your spiritual nourishment.

The physical body cannot travel to the Father's mansions. Remember Jesus said there are many mansions in my Father's House, we know there are at least twelve Heavens, and we learn if we travel to those mansions, those Heavens, we gain incredible experience. My last Zoom talk was "Becoming More Receptive to God's Love." The best way to become more receptive is the HU because Soul can accept more love than your physical self, that is another advantage, so it kind of ties in today. When you HU and you get stronger spiritually Prophet can take you into the Heavens. The best way to experience God's Love is go to the Heavens; the mansions and Heavens where the love is very, very concentrated, and when you keep getting dipped like a candle in that love, it changes you. The love that is down here is just as concentrated, but it is disguised because most people are not prepared; they could not handle that much of God's Love. I can take you as Prophet into the Heavens. But do I take your physical bodies? I cannot do that. But I can take you as Soul but only if Soul is balanced and nourished. So we get a tremendous experience with God's Love, His teachings, all kinds of things, but I can only take you and give you that experience as Soul and only if Soul is reasonably nourished and reasonably woken up. It would not be good for you to take you if you are not nourished. I would not take somebody into the Heavens until they HUed for weeks and months and got that foundation, and then it is a joy to take you. I used to take my students a lot.

On every single Heaven or every mansion there is a Temple of God with a former Prophet who is the guardian, and he is mainly the teacher. When you go to God's churches in Heaven you get His truth and Love. Most churches on the planet have pieces of God's truth, but I do not think there are any that have all the truth. And sometimes mankind with good intention misunderstands or for some reason tweaks the truth. When I take you as Soul into the Heavens, and again that is the operative word, only as Soul not your physical bodies, this is a gigantic advantage when you wake up as Soul you can travel the Heavens with Prophet while you still have a physical body safely sitting in Virginia or wherever. The experiences you gain are priceless. You experience God's Love, we go to God's Temples of Learning, you meet past Prophets that you may have known in former incarnations. You get wisdom directly from God — there is a Holy Book in each temple that is directly from the Heavenly Father to you precisely at that moment. It is not scripture written two thousand years ago, though that is still beautiful, it is right "off the press" literally to each of you personally from the Heavenly Father, and you cannot do that in the physical body. That is one of the advantages of operating as Soul. So you feel His Love and you start learning His ways. His ways are truthfully taught at these Temples. There's nothing man-made in these Temples, only truth. So you learn His ways, His teachings, and you experience His Love.

Another advantage, let me back up a bit. Most of you, if you are not familiar with this, if you read the Bible you read Saint Paul knew a man that was caught up to the third Heaven. Well that is what we do all the time at Guidance for a Better Life retreat center. Saint Paul literally was the one caught up to the third Heaven but not in his physical body. I do not think a Christian ever thinks about that. He did not physically go to the third Heaven; he went as Soul, and the Prophet back then took him up to the third Heaven. He said he knew a man because he did not want to brag; he was humble. And we do that all the time, but we also go up to the twelfth Heaven, the third Heaven, the second Heaven, wherever it is to give you the lesson you need, but again only as Soul and only if you are reasonably nourished. I think most people when they think about Saint Paul going to the third Heaven, I wonder if they just picture him in a physical body going? No. It was only the real Saint Paul not his "Earth suit" but only him as Soul. I hope that this is motivating some of you to make sure you get your daily bread because everything opens up then. So much that is not known to be possible for most of mankind becomes very possible and incredibly advantageous for all kinds of reasons not just an abundant life, to know yourself and also to know God better. And this second thing here is, and this is preposterous to most people, but I think most of you, with very few exceptions, all my students, long time students, have literally left their body in Virginia safe, sitting in our sanctuary, and I can take you as Soul because God allows it. As Soul, the real eternal you, I take you back to your Home where God created you eons ago. Can you imagine the benefit, if you are not sure if God loves you? If there is a God, maybe there's a God, maybe there is not? Can you imagine the benefit if you will get your daily bread of being taken by a Prophet to literally meet face-to-face the Heavenly Father, and He tells you He loves you? That beats a preacher telling you, although that is nice. That experience sure beats reading scripture, which is beautiful. And then you come back and read scripture and scripture comes alive! But the point is only as Soul can you do that, I cannot take you in your physical bodies.

As you nourish Soul your life changes, besides traveling to the Heavens to eventually meet the Heavenly Father when you are prepared, to go to Temples, God's churches in Heaven where you learn His true teachings not polluted in any way purposely or by accident by mankind. Let me read something here from my notes: "Your life seems to flow from these actual experiences in a graceful and peaceful way. You become your real potential." Your magnificent self starts shining through this physical "Earth suit." I wonder if I can get some thumbs-up from my longtime students, is there a certain peace and a grace and a balance in life now that you never had before? Is that true or is that too much? I see a lot of thumbs-up. And you are becoming your true — your true better self, but you cannot become your better self when you do not know who you are, and our physical body is only a small piece, temporary piece of who we are. So when you nourish yourself and get that daily spiritual bread that Jesus talked about, I'm talking about, and all Prophets talk about, if nothing else you start knowing you. And things just start making sense, and there is a peace and grace in life that you did not have before.

Okay. Time's flying. All right, another example, fear of death. A lot of people do not live life with full gusto and really get out and live because they are afraid of dying. When you leave your body as Soul, the real you, many times, you identify that you are Soul and your body is something temporary down here for eighty or so years or whatever maybe longer, but the real you goes on with your thoughts, your opinions, the people you love when you pass on you still love them, you get to watch over them, and when you pass on you get to all meet again, life goes on. That is why the grace and peace come in. There is not much down here that troubles you as much as it used to because you have such a long view. But when we do this many times, for some of you, the fear of death becomes a non-event; there's just no reason to fear death. There is nothing to be afraid of. In fact it's a grand, glorious, beautiful thing when the time is right, let God decide that, but when the time comes it is a stunning experience that you have done so many times. It is a grand experience. You meet your loved ones on the other side, you keep your love for people, you know who you are. You keep your opinions and your thoughts, you keep your uniqueness. So it is nothing to be afraid of.

That is an advantage of operating more as Soul and having these experiences as Soul. If you are somebody that fears death, then you cannot really live life. And in my discourse "Blocks to Spiritual Growth Part One," we talked about this in one of my early Zoom meetings, if you get rid of some of that fear in your heart, you all know you have more room for love. So fear is something that reduces the abundant life. If you get rid of fear by waking up your true self that is also a plus. I hope I'm making a good sales job that it is a really good deal to wake up as Soul, and most people do not, most clergy I do not think understand what Soul really is. That is one advantage of having Prophet mentor you. Operating as Soul and getting your daily bread opens up a whole world that is not open to other people. I hope for those that already appreciate operating as Soul, the word re-appreciate, which we did a discourse on years ago, I hope you re-appreciate and re-emphasize the advantages of staying balanced and nourished.

Past lives. A lot of people do not know, but I think my students know, a lot of your physical ailments and hurts and emotional scars, not all of them, some are from this childhood too, but a lot of them are from past lives. And when you reincarnate you do not have your memories; the physical body does not have memories but Soul does. I can take you back when the Heavenly Father tells me it is time if it will help you in this life, and we heal you of emotional scars and some physical issues from past lives. And all my students have received healings. That is way more effective than just healing issues from this life. Now a lot of you have childhood issues. Many have been damaged in our childhoods I think, that is one thing, but a lot of the deeper emotional issues are from former lives. I cannot take you back physically, I am trying to make that point again, but as Soul that is where your memories are. I may not even have to help you if you stay nourished as Soul and start knowing the real you, sometimes you will start figuring it out on your own, or I will come in a dream, or I will actually take you back in a dream or guided contemplation, not in your body but as Soul, your magnificent eternal self, and you go, "oh that's why I feel that way," or "that is why I cannot stand so and so," or "that is why I'm so afraid of this or that," and we can heal those things. We did this metaphor of a person being a guitar string years ago, where you are a string on a guitar and each fret represents a different lifetime. If we take a kink out of the guitar string just in this lifetime but the guitar string is kinked at another fret, there are still needed healings for an abundant life. Any kink in the string means it does not work correctly. So as Soul we can go back and heal things from former lives for the purpose of making this life better. I hope I'm selling you on the advantages of Soul. I have never worked this hard to encourage you, to show you the stunning advantages. It's like it is almost unfair, if you operate as Soul down here with a Prophet guiding you, if your life does not turn out abundant there is just something wrong. If you cannot find peace and joy and heal some of these old scars, what is your problem?

So, all right. Another thing real quick. Soul received what I call a super-gift. I'll speed up a bit. Soul was given a most amazing gift from God as part of the package we all have. I call this special gift a "truth detector," and God built into Soul, the real you, not your brain not your body, the real you, the ability to know truth even when the mind is not quite convinced. Up at the retreat center I share things that are so far beyond what people have ever heard about, or that any preachers ever talked about, that the only way you could sit in your seats and not freak out and let me really keep teaching you is that gift, and I treasure that gift because it allows me to share things and push the envelope with you. As Soul you know if I am telling you the truth, even when your brain's going, "Whoa what is that?" Or, "I never heard that before!" But you sit there. In your heart, which is Soul, you go, "I know it's true." Otherwise I do not think we would grow as much up at the retreat center because we definitely push the frontier. You hear things that nobody else will teach you and that helps you grow. It is a benefit. So as a teacher without God giving you a truth detector, I would have both my hands tied behind my back, and I'd be hanging upside down trying to teach. I do not think I could get any of you where you are at. To me that is very precious. And I put something in bold so let me read it. **"You have been created with certain attributes, as Soul, to help guide you during your travels. One of the greatest is the ability of Soul to recognize truth when It hears it."** But it only works well if Soul is what? It starts with an "N," nourished. And what if you eat a whole bunch of food one day, then you do not eat for a month, then you eat a whole bunch. How about consistently in a reasonably balanced way, consistently nourished? It will change your life. I see Michelle, I think you HU regularly, and you can share later if we have time, I think it is literally changing your life because the real you that has so much knowledge and wisdom and experience is starting to guide your decisions. A nourished Soul is a big part of good decision-making.

Okay you still want more? Have I proved it yet or do I have to keep selling, selling, and selling? All right, let me do a little more. I make note cards so I'm going to use them. I might save this till later ... I want to talk about one of the, what I believe is the Fourth Commandment. I was asked to make it the Fourth Commandment, certain Prophets make certain teachings of God commandments at His request. The Fourth Commandment is to be a coworker with God. That is probably the most satisfying thing a Soul could ever achieve, to be a helper for God. It is called a coworker, and we also call it a servant of God. Jesus says service is its own reward, boy was that an understatement. And when you serve God to help His other children and bless His other children by letting God use us as a coworker, it is one of the highest achievements of Soul, and once you get there as Soul you can maintain that for lifetimes. Once a Prophet or you get to that level of service you generally are a coworker with God for eternity, and that level is where most of my students are now at. I'm trying to get them to that level of permanence.

A lot of people are so obsessed with service they do not realize they are going in the wrong direction and to me it is a negative; it's not a positive. It is a positive that they have the desire and heart to serve, but it sometimes throws them out of balance. If they are good people with good intentions, they most likely will not harm anyone. We do not want to be servers we want to be coworkers, and the primary difference is a coworker listens to God and passes on NOT what they think is best but instead what God knows someone needs. God will always know better than us what another child of His needs most. It takes more than just a physical body to become a coworker. The physical body can pass on the results of coworking and talk to people and listen to people and look at people with love and all that, but knowing what is God's will for someone takes coworking with God through His Prophet. Soul is the primary part of us that can become a coworker because only the real you as Soul can have that precise communication with the Heavenly Father through His Prophet. A coworker is somebody really in tune with what God is suggesting through His Holy Spirit, what He is saying moment to moment, precisely, what is absolutely the best thing for that other child of God. If we love other Souls we too want the very best for them so rather than guessing someone's needs, we listen to or ask God through His Prophet what to do. Achieving this level of inner communication brings great joy. So coworking is also service, but service is not necessarily coworking with the Divine.

So my students are hesitant coworkers, and we focus on hesitant. Why hesitant? Is it because they do not really want to serve but if they have to? They do not want to serve on weekends, only nine to five? Only if it's kind of fun, not if it is harsh news? No, they are hesitant coworkers because they want to make absolutely certain they are "hearing" what the will is of the Father through Prophet for that person. They do not want to go off half-cocked and do something for that person that they think the person needs. Most of the time that is not doing harm, but it is just kind of a guess; it may not be what the person needs. The Heavenly Father knows us really well, and He certainly knows what somebody you are talking to needs far more than any of us would know. I do not really know what you all need if I do not listen to the Heavenly Father. As Prophet, everything I pass on I try to get from the Heavenly Father; otherwise, it would not be worth coming up to the retreat center. It would just be some guy talking. And I am training my students to be coworkers, and they are, almost all of them have been ordained by the Heavenly Father; you are ordained as Soul, and only Soul is refined enough to be able to be a coworker. So somebody that is extremely obsessed with service to me is a liability; they are a danger to themselves and others. Now that means they have a good heart so they have good potential, and I would be happy to help them become a coworker, but they need to throttle down and learn how to be a coworker to help somebody with what the Father wants, not what they think is good. None of us are that smart but God is. But to be a coworker, and I do not know if you think about this, our bodies are the speaker system. We pass it on, the message, but where do we get the precise message? From Prophet, and I get it from the Heavenly Father. You, the eternal you is Soul, that is the real coworker and that is the part He ordained. Now we need our bodies to give people information, to talk to them, to comfort, to hold their hands, to give them a hug, whatever, but the wisdom and the clarity of what that person needs, if you really care about somebody, you want what God wants for them not what you think is best. Service is giving them what you think best, coworking is giving what God wants for them. And somebody that is too excited about being a servant has great potential, but they are frankly a liability at first. So my students are hesitant coworkers not because they do not want to serve, they cannot wait to serve because service is a stunning joy, it's the most satisfying thing I think we can do, but we hesitate to make sure. We just slow down a moment: Is this what God wants, the Divine wants for a person we are being used to bless? And sometimes you might know, but we want the best for these other children of God, and only you as Soul, that is nourished, can provide that.

Let's review Soul, your magnificent eternal self. Soul is an individualized piece of God's Voice, the Holy Spirit, therefore you are divine. Does that mean you act divine very often? Maybe not, but nonetheless you are all divine, and over time you can see it in my students, you can see the divine in them, and that is also your potential. You are a divine child of God, and it is stunning if you really let that sink in. As Soul you have existed for a long, long, long time, I really do not know how long. I hate to put a number on it, hundreds of thousands of years? I do not know, but you will continue on for eternity as Soul. You are literally eternal, and that is as Soul. Below the fifth Heaven Soul enters a body, an outer sheath. When your physical body wears out in sixty, eighty, one hundred years normally, sometimes sooner, the real you continues on and on and on, and all your experiences you retain as Soul. The people you love when you pass on, Soul still loves them. Your relationship with Prophet, all your growth as Soul, you can hang on to. The growth in the physical body, say you work out every day and you're in super shape, eventually, no matter what you do that good conditioning and those rock-hard abs are going to dissipate, so it's not eternal. So if you want to invest in a long-term investment that will definitely make a difference in your life, you want to invest every day in getting your daily spiritual bread so that the eternal part of you, that divine part, becomes more operational. And I hope I convinced you of all the benefits, and I just scratched the surface on that.

So this is my view, it may or may not be yours, to not put your spiritual growth into a place of high importance delays your opportunity to go Home to the Heavenly Father. You will never take your physical body Home, but Soul can go back someday and live with the Heavenly Father, after a long cycle down here many, many thousands of years and lifetimes, and I am preparing some of my students to be able, if they choose, to go all the way back Home. They are now spiritually mature, they are coworkers with God. They have earned the right to go to the Heavenly Father, or come back down here because they want to serve as coworkers. To me putting your spiritual growth at a very high level of importance in life is very important. That may not be for everybody. And to do that, when you have the advantage of nourishing Soul, life really starts working for your benefit and the benefit of others around you. And as Prophet, God ordained me to help Souls, to prepare you and to show you your eternal self. I do not believe any preacher or clergy does that, but Prophets prepare you to go Home not in your body but as Soul and also to help you have an abundant life while you are living here. You might as well have a great life while you are here. And I think those of you that consistently nourish Soul and have been spiritually woken up, and had all these great experiences I talked about, I would say all of you have a more abundant, more balanced, joyful life. And you see from such a high view now, you almost see through eternity. You see through a lot of the frustrations and the challenges down here, and the endless births and deaths, and this round and around we go on a merry-go-round down here. I think a lot of things that trouble people down here, that bother them so much, I think at a certain point as Soul, if well nourished and has experiences like I talked about, these frustrations that bother most people, I think most of you can stay above the fray that a lot of people simply cannot do, and this ability adds peace and joy to your life when up above the constant fray on Earth.

My job is to train coworkers not servants but coworkers for God. That is my primary job and to prepare my students, longtime students, to literally complete this cycle where you were sent down here as a gift of love when you were a baby as Soul and all these lifetimes. I tend to be the one that polishes you for that final growth where you can go home to the Father, as many of you already have. I want to read something I wrote: **"When the mind** … [this physical part of us], when the mind and all its aspects within the human self have come under control of the individual Soul there is a new type of person." They are now ruled by Soul, and I think most my students are, and can view life, all life from this lofty position. I want to share another scripture quote that I love and Del my son loves it particularly. So what is your potential as Soul? We kind of talked about you as Soul, but I love this; it is the real you, your future. "Soul's future is the future of a thing whose growth and splendor has no limits." That's a mouthful. Now physically we have limits: we can only jump so high, no matter how smart you are you do not know everything, no matter how much you work out your body eventually deteriorates, you can lift weights but you cannot lift but so much. We have limits; as Soul we do not have those limits. So I find that statement, "Soul's future is the future of a thing whose growth ..." Soul grows also, you remember you are down here to grow and mature, so Soul grows, but It does not grow when It is asleep. That is another reason you need to wake It up. Your potential is growth and splendor with no limits, and I hope that sinks in. So I hope I made a case that if you just operate in your physical body and do the best you can, you are so handicapped compared to doing the best you can in your body but also growing as Soul. It is almost unfair living down here when you wake up Soul. Everything you see so different, and see more as it really truly is. So another way to look at Soul, Soul is boundless and can experience freedom beyond what I want to share today. You can be a billionaire and think you are free or live in a free country; Soul has the freedom to travel the Heavens, to see life through thousands of years, beyond the daily frustrations. So that is a whole other topic I may share someday. You become so extraordinarily free at a level most people cannot comprehend as you nourish and wake up Soul. But it all starts with what? What is the beginning of this whole thing? You must wake Soul up by getting your daily spiritual bread, and it should be a joy to get your daily bread, to sing HU, it should be something you look forward to; it should not be like taking out the trash. And once you catch the spirit of this, life can be really good down here in a physical body; we can treasure our bodies, enjoy them, but we are so much more. So I think that is enough on "Your Magnificent Eternal Self" today. God loves you and I love you, and I appreciate you all so much. May the blessings be, and may you receive some pearl of wisdom today that improves your life. Thank you.

Prophet Del Hall

January 2, 2021

Part Two: YouTube Audience Comments

This *Zoom With Prophet* talk was published on my YouTube channel for my viewers. Following are selected comments that I thought you, the reader, might find interesting and benefit from. I believe these comments add some additional clarity and provide a personal perspective on the topic of "Your Magnificent Eternal Self."

Thank you, Prophet, for teaching us Soul is made out of God's Love. Hearing this description of Soul brought up feelings different from hearing Soul is made from the Holy Spirit, God's Light and Sound. I felt more connected to my Heavenly Father hearing how my eternal self is made out of His Love. Knowing I am made from God's Love leaves me desiring even more to demonstrate gratitude for this gift through growing and nourishing my eternal self whether through singing HU or through other means of nourishing Soul. If Soul is made out of God's Love it therefore follows Its growth and splendor has no limits, for God's Love, as I understand it, has no limits either. Thank you!

Roland Vonder Muhll

Roland, I am happy this way of describing the Holy Spirit, God's Voice, was helpful to you. Blessings, Del

Guidance for a Better Life

Dear Prophet, I loved how you explained our uniqueness as Soul, that even though we are all made from the same raw material, we are so very unique after many lifetimes of experiences. It gave me the image of stones in a stream: they're all basically the same raw material, but all different and unique after many years of water flowing around them. After a long time it makes stones with very different shapes and textures and colors, and each beautifully different in its own right. The uniqueness that the river of life creates in us is stunning! Thank you for this beautiful image of Soul. It also makes me appreciate the little and unique things in life, that there's beauty in little details, and that God loves that.

Jorge Carrizosa

I love your stones in the river story! Thank you for your comment Jorge. Blessings, Del

Guidance for a Better Life

Thank you Prophet for sharing all this wisdom and profound truth about our eternal selves called "Soul." How you describe Soul, the real us, is so very beautiful; God created us, Soul, from His divine Essence. We are an individualized piece of His Holy Spirit, Light and Sound, His Love, created out of His Voice, and we are divine and holy! Seeing ourselves (and others) as a beautiful piece of divine spirit rather than this physical body or "Earth suit" we reside in, opens us up to recognizing the true beauty in God's Love for all His children. We are made in the image of God, as radiant light and sound! It's really amazing! Stunning, as you said! I love your view on our uniqueness; how God invented & specializes in uniqueness, and how our spiritual experiences as Soul adds to our individual uniqueness. I am so grateful to You for teaching me that I am Soul, and eternal, and for helping me "wake up" to grow the eternal side of myself. Learning to identify more and more with this part of the real me, and experiencing myself as Soul has given me a freeing and peaceful perspective, which is much different from how I was taught and lived earlier in life. It certainly rang true for me when you said churches on Earth have pieces of God's truth, but not all the truth. You have taught me spiritual truths no clergy could teach me, all which ring true as Soul. It is true when given experiences as Soul, fear of death vanishes. This, in and of itself, is miraculous; I have been freed immensely. I hope your viewers recognize what an amazing gift it is to be able to grow the eternal part of ourselves, and come to know the great benefits to being "woken up," being spiritually nourished, becoming spiritually mature, and operating as Soul which opens up a whole new way of living, learning, gaining wisdom, accepting love, and experiencing God's never-ending and sacred love. I thank God for sending You, His chosen Prophet, to help prepare us as Soul to go Home, and for showing me my eternal self. Thank you for imparting spiritual truth on the Magnificence of Soul, and so much more.

Moira Crodelle

Moira thank you for your very complete and comprehensive comment, and you are welcome. Blessings, Del

Guidance for a Better Life

Thank you! This was such a clear and comprehensive discussion on this topic that I never heard in the many years attending church in my earlier life. It's a benefit in itself to recognize myself as Soul, that alone changes how I view life, but then all the extraordinary benefits there are to operating as Soul, wow. It makes sense that in order to operate as Soul I have to get daily spiritual nourishment — daily bread for that eternal part of me to wake up and get strong enough to activate and have access to all the magnificent qualities God created me with. I also heard things in a new and fresh way in this video that helped me better understand, internalize, and appreciate that when operating as Soul I also have access to all the wisdom and learning that I gained through many lifetimes of experiences. I knew those were a part of me at some level, but I received a lot more clarity on just how present and operational that wisdom and experience can be in daily life when operating as Soul. It's like that eternal part of us, Soul, leaves a great spiritual inheritance, an inheritance given to us from our Heavenly Father that accumulates with each lifetime through lessons of living and learning His ways, and we get to reclaim it in the next incarnation — if we wake up and operate as Soul. That is amazing! Thank you for helping me wake up Prophet and teaching me so I can claim my spiritual inheritance, enjoy the God-given splendors of Soul, and continue to grow.

Lorraine F

I like how you shared the idea of "spiritual inheritance" when your eternal self receives Its daily spiritual bread. Blessings, Del

Guidance for a Better Life

Knowing we are Soul that has a physical body, not the opposite, is incredibly eye opening and liberating, and explains so many of life's mysteries. Over time and with your teaching and guidance I have come to accept this profound truth about myself and others, and the more I have learned from you and grown in this area, the happier and freer I have become, until I almost don't recognize who I used to be. This is an amazing discourse which not only explains who we really are, but also offers useful insights and suggestions on how to manifest our divine nature and live as our true, magnificent, eternal selves, Soul. I believe there is no other teaching on the planet that breaks this down and explains it in such an accurate, thorough and practical way. Thank you, Prophet for making this beautiful and sacred wisdom available to all!

Laurence Elder

You are welcome Laurence, and thank you for your comment. Blessings, Del

Guidance for a Better Life

At a young age I had a strong feeling there had to be more to life than what I could see. I recall looking into my own eyes reflecting back at me in a handheld mirror wondering what was behind them. I often wondered about two things, who am I and why am I here? The religious leaders in the church taught me I was born with a Soul. I learned very little about this mysterious part of me and without getting into church doctrine, simply put, I was taught the Souls of good people go to Heaven when they die and the Souls of bad people go to Hell. The idea there just had to be more to life than what could be seen stayed with me until eventually my need for answers turned into a sincere prayer to know more about the purpose and meaning for my existence. God was listening, heard my prayer, and through a series of events he led me to Prophet Del Hall's school. The first time I listened to Prophet teach, an inner knowing rose up within me and I realized he knew what I was seeking. Prophet's words brought relief to my heart as he confirmed what Soul knew all along. Yes, there is a whole lot more to our lives than what can be seen with physical eyes. Singing HU is one of the first things I learned from Prophet and I sing it every day. It is a beautiful way to demonstrate love and express gratitude to God for all He does for me and for those I know and care about. I know from my own personal experience, singing HU with a grateful heart nourishes Soul and helps open the channels of inner communication with the Holy Spirit. There is a link with divine guidance which is available to assist in all areas of life when we put our attention on spirit and make following God's ways a priority. Prophet's program of study and his discourses help expand my point of view. He provides spiritual experiences to sharpen one's awareness of their authentic self and slowly wake up Soul. There are subtle changes taking place at the very heart of me as I more fully realize and integrate the truth of what I am, where I came from, and my purpose for being. I have come to accept this is true: God knows me and is not disappointed in me. This insight has allowed me to forgive myself for errors in judgment made earlier in life when I was spiritually immature and not yet ready or able to access the innate divine qualities of Soul lying dormant and waiting to be activated. There is now more peace in my heart, more patience for myself, more compassion for others, and my days abound with joy! I am grateful for the opportunity to be taught by Prophet Del. I am thankful he shares his love, wisdom, knowledge, and experience with us. I love you Prophet.

Bernadette Spitale

Thank you Bernadette for your beautiful comment, I hope it helps others. Blessings, Del

Guidance for a Better Life

Part Three: Disciple Testimonies

I am including some testimonies from my disciples on the topic of your eternal self, Soul. These personal stories are written by individuals who have experienced themselves as Soul many times, most of whom operate as Soul a majority of the time. This greatly enriches the quality of their lives and blesses the lives of their loved ones too. I hope these testimonies provide additional clarity and deeper understanding on this important topic. They are proof that living more free and in peace is possible.

Precious and Beautiful in God's Eyes

Soul truly equals Soul in Its divinity and in God's love for It, but countless lifetimes of experience have made us into truly unique spiritual beings. This amazing testimony of being "beheld" by the Heavenly Father demonstrates this beautifully.

For years, Prophet has taught us that Soul equals Soul and we are all made out of the same raw material — God's Light and Sound. I have been blessed to have been taken spiritually to the Heavens where I witnessed not only myself as Soul but have also seen and experienced the stunning beauty, joy, wisdom, and freedom in other Souls as well. While we all "looked" similar during these inner journeys, each Soul was distinct. Like Prophet Del Hall says in his video "Your Magnificent Eternal Self" Soul's uniqueness is so much more profound than our nationality, skin color, whether we are male or female, or what society sees as uniqueness. God sees us differently than the surface sheath we see when we look in the mirror.

Over the years as Prophet's student, I have witnessed his love and genuine appreciation for our uniqueness as Soul. This was not something he just said, but something he demonstrated in how he spoke to us, how he treated each person, how he met and valued each Soul where they were, and how he demonstrated support and interest in the things that mattered to us. I know without a doubt that Heavenly Father truly loves and cherishes us too. Our long life as Soul, spread into hundreds of different lifetimes, makes each of us unique. These experiences help shape who we are — our interests, our sense of humor (or lack thereof), our likes and dislikes, and our disposition. This has helped me to understand why I felt immediately connected to and familiar with various people throughout my life as well as my interests or fascination with certain time periods in history. Our unique environments not only from childhood but from many lifetimes, our joys and our challenges, and many growth opportunities shaped who we are today. There is a profound beauty in that diversity, yet we all share the same Creator.

On one inner journey guided by Prophet, I was spiritually brought Home to our Heavenly Father with the sacred privilege of witnessing how He sees me, up close and personal. This may seem preposterous, too wonderful to be true, but I assure you it is true. We had sung the glorious love song to God, HU, and now I knelt before our Heavenly Father with Prophet beside me. As I looked to my side, I saw many, many Souls also kneeling in reverence. While we looked similar on the surface as vibrating and living balls of God's Light and Sound, each Soul was distinct. I recognized my husband and my friend through knowingness, even though they looked similar on the surface. While we are all cut from the same cloth — GOD'S LOVE — Soul is still unique and has distinct qualities, interests, and abilities.

Then we were invited and given the opportunity to move into the Hand of God. I felt so loved and secure, God's Love surrounding and filling every fiber of my being. I had no needs that were unmet, nothing to crave, everything I could ever need or want was already here in that sacred moment in God's Hand. Then His Hand started to rise upward. As Soul, I knew I was going to be lifted before God's Face. I could feel His breath wash over and into me. I could feel His Love wash over and into me. Before I met His gaze, I instinctively felt the desire to be known, to be seen, to be utterly transparent before my Heavenly Father. He already knew and saw me anyway, but the desire to open up and be witnessed welled up inside me, like a response to what was about to happen. Then He beheld me, with such a tenderness, such a sincere appreciation for His creation. I knew I was precious to Him, as is each and every Soul. He was not just seeing the surface of who I am as Soul but all of me, and He loved what He saw. The physical body, no matter how beautiful, pales in comparison to the beauty and splendor of Soul. After this precious moment passed, I was changed. To be completely seen and beheld and still be precious and beautiful to our Heavenly Father allowed a greater love and healthy appreciation for my own uniqueness to grow over time. It did not come all in one moment but has been building now for years, changing how I treat myself and the peace I have in truly being me.

In order to grow, Soul needs experiences and this takes time. Our Heavenly Father doesn't expect us to have it all figured out but gives us time to mature and grow. The immense privilege to have had this experience of being brought before God and being seen has transformed me. It has given me a greater appreciation for my uniqueness as Soul as well as loving and appreciating those around me even more deeply for their individuality. It has changed how I see others on daily errands. It does not matter if their physical form is old or young, large or small, nor if it seemingly has "imperfections" from the human lens — the innate beauty is still there. This does not mean I have to like everyone though. To my eyes the beauty is still somewhere in there, even if it is buried.

There are actions that are wrong, and we are held accountable with consequences to help us grow, but God still loves Soul. It takes time to mature, and it takes much more time to activate and be operational as Soul in our daily life on Earth. But wherever we are in our process of unfolding, God loves and cherishes our individuality and beauty as Soul. What a gift to see and know this to be true.

Written by Molly Comfort

My First Glimpse of Soul

Our true identity as Soul is hidden behind our earthly packaging and its shortcomings. We are so much more than our physical bodies and minds; we are Soul, eternal spiritual beings created out of the Light and Love of God. Being able to accept and live this truth is a cornerstone to spiritual freedom. It is one of the first things Prophet teaches and helps his students experience for themselves.

The first time I visually saw my true and eternal self, Soul, I was surprised. In my ignorance I thought I knew what Soul would look like. I was at a special weeklong retreat at Guidance for a Better Life. In a contemplation led by Prophet Del Hall, I was taken out of my body spiritually. The contemplation was an active experience where I was allowed to see and know real truths, God's truths.

It was pleasantly dark all around me; at least that was what I was aware of. I knew Prophet was by my side. I was given a special mirror that would show me what I looked like spiritually as Soul. I thought I would see a soft white orb of light. I spiritually raised the mirror up to eye level and looked. I saw a flash of dazzling, brilliant light. It was so vibrant! It was so much brighter than the glint off a diamond in the sun. In that instant I experienced some of my God-given qualities of life, motion, and beauty all at once.

Prophet thank you so much for that first glimpse of the real me, Soul. It was so far removed from the angry, confused person I thought I was. I thank you Prophet for the truth that I can operate and see with Soul's viewpoint, a much higher and more peaceful view of life. I do not have to live every day in the human consciousness of anger, fear, guilt, and unworthiness. I can now recognize and learn to live with love from a higher spiritual view!

I work in a hospital emergency department. Driving home from a long shift last week I was reveling in the remembrance of a discourse Del, the current Prophet, gave about the truth of Soul. As I drove I was in a sea of God's Light and Sound. This Divine light and love flowed all around, and Its beauty inspired a subtle and deep joy within my heart. I was filled with love. At that moment I was experiencing that as Soul, I was an individualized part of this light and sound, the very Essence of God. I appreciated knowing you Prophet, the one who speaks truth and shares God's Living Word with Soul. It is such a privilege to know you Prophet and know the reality of God.

Written by Carmen Snodgrass

Child of God — Really

You are so much more than your temporal physical body. You are Soul, an eternal child of God, created out of the Light of God. Many find this hard to believe but nonetheless, it is true. Beneath our shortcomings as humans, we are spiritually magnificent. The more you allow the Prophet to let you experience, know, and identify with your true self, Soul, the more the "earthly baggage" will lose its grip.

We gathered at the Guidance for a Better Life retreat center, ready to sing HU. Del explained the HU and then said that you might know intellectually that you are a child of God but not fully understand what exactly that means, how sacred and special that really is. In time and with spiritual experience you may gain true understanding. I thought I knew what it meant to be a child of God but wondered if I was about to learn more.

During the quiet time after singing HU, I flew rapidly through a narrow dim tunnel and came out at God's Ocean. I recognized this as the twelfth Heaven, one of the very high Heavenly Worlds. I was distinctly aware that I was Soul. Instead of a body, I was my true self, a ball of light. I sparkled with pure rays of white light. Within my light was nothing dark or negative. I knew intuitively that it would be impossible for anything negative to stick to Soul.

When I had exited the tunnel, I escaped the bodies that cover Soul and disguise the perfection of God's creation. The disguise is so good that it even fools us. Anger, fear, worry, and their relations are not Soul. We are not our defilements or our mistakes. We are children of God, perfectly created with virtually limitless potential. As I looked out at the water I recognized sparkles in it made of the same light as me. God created Soul out of Itself, in Its image, Its own Light. Yet I also recognized that God is much more than Soul could ever be, even if Soul's potential was fully realized.

I was not alone. Prophet brought me there and remained beside me. As a ball of light he embraced me, his light enveloping mine.

Within him, I felt closer to God, with all that God knows and sees at the Prophet's fingertips. I cannot find my way home alone. I need a guide, the Prophet, to show me the way.

As I opened my eyes following the HU, the world looked different. I knew deeper than before that I am Soul, a child of God. Beneath our human coverings is Soul, my true self and yours. We are both, you and I, one of God's glorious creations. Sing HU, look within, and ask the Prophet to show you your true self. A grand adventure awaits!

Written by Jean Enzbrenner

I Am Light and Sound

A core truth you will come across in our writings time and time again is that you do not have a Soul, rather... you are Soul that has a body. You are an eternal spiritual being within a temporal earthly embodiment. This seemingly simple switch in perspective can have a monumental effect on how you see yourself.

I returned home one Sunday evening in 2014 from a winter weekend retreat with a strong desire in my heart. I wanted to let my love for the eternal spiritual teachings consume me in every area of inner and outer life and had a willingness and commitment to go to a whole new level in my spiritual journey. Prophet's words during the weekend were etched in my heart, "Immerse yourself in It" (meaning Divine Spirit and the ways of the eternal). "Let your excitement for these teachings spill out. If you have the eye of the tiger in you, let it loose." His words reverberated in me and brought a boldness and confidence going forward, exploring the inner worlds with him in new ways, being open to new opportunities to share the love and wisdom in these teachings with others, and approaching my time spent in contemplation, dreaming, and reading with creativity and renewed purpose.

The night after I returned from this retreat I spent time in contemplation just before bed and lovingly sang, "Prophet." Prophet is my beloved inner and outer teacher, God's ordained representative on Earth who is here to show us how to have a more personal relationship with our Heavenly Father and guide us home to Him. From personal experience I know him as the embodiment of the Holy Spirit, the Light and Sound of God, who physically manifests the fullness of God's Love, wisdom, and other glories of the Divine, and the one who can help us manifest this same Divine nature that is in all of us. After singing Prophet's name, I sang HU, an ancient name for God. I imagined breathing in light and sound, the Breath of God. I breathed in deeply, holding it a little then slowly breathing out as I sang, sending love back to God freshened and enriched with light and sound each time. I was suddenly inspired to say, "I am light and sound." Soul is made of light and sound, a part of Divine Spirit, a "spark" of God. A big growth area over the years has been learning to accept I am Soul, but in this moment even that was holding back the fullness of the truth I was hungry for, "I am light and sound." Wow, that was a bold statement! But, that was what was in my heart so I sang it aloud, a little shy and hesitant at first and then with more and more confidence. These words resonated at a deep level. By stating this truth more directly, I identified with my true nature more than I ever had before.

I was taken by Prophet to an inner spiritual Heaven where I stood next to a brilliant beam of flowing light and sound. I knew this beam as an aspect of the inner Prophet. I felt myself as a "strand" of this beam but separate and distinct as I stood next to it. I then saw an aspect of God Himself there with us, one I knew personally and loved with everything I am. I continued to sing HU. The air I breathed came direct from God. His breaths came into me and became my breath that felt like a river coursing through me. I then saw His breath was also giving life to the beam. His breath became the beam itself. As I continued to send love to God by singing HU, I moved closer and closer to the beam of God's Light and Sound until I was inside of It. It began then to flow through me. My perception of this grew slowly until I could feel a steady flow of Divine Spirit running through my being. I could still feel myself, but I no longer felt separate. I was inside of It, and now I was aware that It was inside of me, flowing continuously, filling me with life and love. I was available to be used for Divine purpose and to be a blessing to others, a willing distributor of God's Light and Sound. Every breath I took connected me back to the Source of all that I saw and knew.

After this inner experience, I remained in quiet contemplation a little longer then went to bed, asking Prophet to guide me as we continued to explore the inner worlds while my physical body slept. When I awoke, I lay in that sacred space and could still feel the light and sound running through me. It brought expanded awareness and insights on the experience itself, dreams from the previous night, interests in daily life, and some home projects that were important to me. These insights gently flowed into my consciousness and then moved along in the river of Divine Spirit that ran through me. I am light and sound! What an incredible gift not just to say these words but to know them from real experience! I was so filled with appreciation and love that I got up after a time and wrote this amazing experience in my journal so I would always remember it.

Prophet blessed me with this gift of love not only to help me more fully manifest my Divine nature, but so I may share it with others. You too can sing this, for it is true for you. You are Soul. You are light and sound. Sing the name "Prophet" and ask his help in getting to know the real you. I guarantee you will like what you see!

Written by Lorraine Fortier

Truth Uncovered

You are so much more than your physical body or any of the labels you could place on yourself. You are first and foremost Soul, an eternal spiritual being created by God with love. If you are blessed to experience this truth firsthand for yourself, you will truly know God loves you just the way you are.

Sometimes we have an experience with God that is pivotal to our growth, a precious moment we hold sacred in our hearts that we will never forget. A moment that transforms us so much we can never see ourselves the way we were before that precious experience. This story is one of those moments for me.

It was the October 3-Day Retreat of 2013. I had been having some inner struggles with self-doubt, self-acceptance, and wondering if God really could love me the way I was. I didn't even know if I loved me just the way I was. We sat in the Beach House, our sacred classroom. It was evening, and even though the wind was blowing cold outside it was warm inside and there was a comforting feeling inside the classroom. Del, the Prophet, offered us the opportunity to be blessed by the Divine and join him for a spiritual experience. As I sat with my eyes closed Prophet led us in a HU song to God. I began to feel lighter, and as I surrendered to the Divine, I felt God's pure Love pouring into me and filling me with attributes such as strength and a trust not only in Him but in myself as well.

I was standing in a huge column of God's Light and Love. I felt completely safe and secure bathed in this love. Prophet showed me myself. I looked how I know myself to look when I look into the mirror; I saw my physical body. Prophet shared with us that we could shed our outer body, our "Earth suit," in the same fashion we would take off a garment of clothing. Prophet helped me shed this outer sheath like a jacket, and I watched it fall away from me. Then without pausing he brought me up to the first Heaven, also referred to as the Astral plane. The part of myself I could now see looked like the physical body I knew as myself, but it was lighter, glowed more, and had a translucency my physical body did not have.

While I did not see Prophet at that moment, I was acutely aware of his strong presence and knew it was only with his guidance and help I was being raised in consciousness to other planes; to higher and higher Heavens. I have read in scripture, 2 Corinthians 12:2 KJV, where Saint Paul spoke of "a man caught up to the third heaven," and this was what I was being given the opportunity to experience for myself. Prophet brought me to the next Heaven, the Causal plane, and on the way up I shed my Astral body and watched it fall away, revealing my Causal body which was even lighter and brighter than my Astral body had been. We continued our upward journey in this beam of God's Light, and as we raised up to each Heaven I shed each corresponding body: my Astral body, my Causal body, my Mental body, and finally I shed my body from the Etheric plane to reveal my true self, Soul. I was a blindingly bright ball of God's Light and Sound.

Prophet asked us to look at our true self. I saw something so beautiful, so pure, and so refined. My brightness and light was astoundingly breathtaking. This is how God made me, this is the real me! I felt no worries, no fears, no concerns, nor insecurities as I basked in this moment of truth experienced. An overwhelming knowing came over me and sank into my heart; God truly does love me. I knew God Himself was placing this truth directly into my open heart: "God loves me just the way I am." I looked at myself, and I loved what I beheld. How could I not love such a precious, beautiful Soul? How could I not love something God uniquely and purposely made? I then understood that those garments, those light-bodies from each Heaven of God covered up my true self, Soul. These light-bodies, layer over layer, had hidden from me the most beautiful truth of all, that I am Soul. This experience completely shattered the previous perception I had of myself.

I wish I could fully convey to you how precious and amazing it was to see myself in my true form as Soul. It was liberating, it was strengthening, and it was awe-inspiring. It freed me from the restrictive confines of how this physical world dictates to me daily that I was a woman, a wife, a mother, a daughter, a worker, and a washer of sippy cups. I am no longer bound by some idea of who I am based on my appearance, or what I do, or my physical belongings. These physical trappings cannot even touch the sacredness of my true Divine nature.

I am so eternally grateful to have been given such a loving gift, to see with clarity how limitless and breathtaking my true self is as Soul. I now have a new image of myself. No wonder I had a hard time loving myself; I had never truly experienced the real me. Do you desire to experience your true self?

Written by Ahna Spitale

Captain's Chair

God created us to live our lives from the higher dynamic viewpoint of Soul, not the lower rigid mental state. Until our mind is on board with this arrangement and takes a backseat to Soul, it will throw quite a fuss. No better is the difference between mind and Soul and the battle for top dog illustrated than in this testimony.

Our family had just finished a delicious evening meal and were enjoying some quality time together in the living room. I had settled into my chair, put my feet up to relax after a day at work, and was enjoying watching our two-year-old daughter play. My wife and I began to share our day when our daughter got up from playing, came over, and told me to get up out of my chair.

I explained to her I was enjoying sitting in my chair. She then got very animated and put her hands under my legs trying her best to lift me out of my chair and said, "Up Daddy!" I firmly told her this was my chair, and I was not moving. She then began to cry and throw a tantrum screaming "My chair Daddy." My wife and I looked at each other with disbelief and a slight smile for this was an exceptional two-year-old moment, even for her, and not her normal behavior. I did not know why, but felt a strong urge to stay firm no matter what she did and stay sitting in my chair. I knew it was best for her. I proceeded to explain to her this was Daddy's chair, but she could sit with me if she liked. She screamed louder, and the tears were running down both sides of her now-flushed red cheeks as she stood there crying and screaming over and over, "Get up Daddy, it is my chair, get up Daddy, it is my chair. Get up Daddy, it is my chair." After about five minutes of this behavior there was no sign of letting up, so my wife took our daughter for a bath to calm her down.

This caught my attention for this was over the top behavior even for a two-year-old child. I was left with a sense of peace. I had a knowing that being firm in my attitude, that I was not going to get up no matter what, was best for all involved. Our daughter got her bath, calmed down, and we all went about our evening.

A few weeks later Prophet was helping me and a group of students understand more about our true nature as Soul. A smile came across my face as the memories of my daughter's behavior a few weeks earlier came rushing into my consciousness. I was given the clarity to see how it tied into our conversation, and it reminded me of a spiritual truth Del has taught me over the years. Soul belongs in charge of our mind and not the other way around. Soul belongs in the captain's chair of our life. We are Soul, the spiritual adult in the relationship with the mind. It is much like the loving relationship between a parent and a child.

The mind, we call the "lower self," is much like a two-year-old and was never designed to run our life. The mind is very limited and is the source of our frustrations, fears, anger, worries, self-doubts, vanity, excessive attachments, and a variety of other ailments. It does not like change, gets overwhelmed, and is generally closed to ideas outside of itself.

These are all traits of the mind but not of Soul. The mind is good at balancing our checkbooks and taking care of our daily tasks, but it is very limited when compared to the boundlessness of Soul.

Soul is creative, resilient, happy, peaceful, and cherishes freedom. It also has clarity, a can-do attitude, access to wisdom, and is generally open to new ideas. Soul has a higher spiritual consciousness than the mind, thus better equipped to run our lives. Soul is free to travel the Heavens, has a greater capacity to give and receive love, and Its potential for growth has no limits.

When we begin to be more spiritually nourished, Soul grows stronger in our life. We begin to make better choices and decisions that benefit us and those we love. Some of the things that help Soul grow stronger are singing HU, reading scriptures, paying attention to dreams, spending time with Prophet, and learning to recognize and be grateful for the blessings in life.

When Soul begins to get stronger the mind may start to protest. At first it feels threatened and does not want to give up sitting in the captain's chair. The lower self has been used to being in charge of our life and has grown to like telling us how things should be. Initially the mind does not like the idea of Soul being in charge and will protest, yell, and scream, much like a two-year-old throwing tantrums to get its way. When Soul gains enough strength It takes charge of the mind and takes Its rightful place in the captain's chair of our life. This is what is best for us, and what is best for our little-self.

Our true self, Soul, is designed by God to be in charge of the mind. Soul has a higher view of life, sees more clearly, and is receptive to God's Love, truth, and guidance. As Soul we are more relaxed, peaceful, joyous, loving, wise, and creative. God actually created the mind to be subservient to Soul; an instrument to be used by Soul to achieve Its purpose during Its sojourn on planet Earth. This experience is a reminder to me that I want to live my life with Soul in charge of the lower self. I want to be nourished as Soul daily and feed It the spiritual food It needs to grow stronger and stay strong, because this is my Divine nature — Soul. It is the true expression of myself as God created me.

Thank you Prophet for giving me this experience and for helping me manifest my Divine nature and the dreams of my heart.

Written by Mark Snodgrass

Through the Eyes of Soul

Whether physically young or old, we are all first and foremost Soul — eternal spiritual beings. We are all children of God. When Soul tunes in spiritually It has a higher view regardless of the physical age of the body Soul resides in.

The room was filled with more than just physical bodies seated in chairs, but Souls that love God. Looking down the rows everyone seemed appreciative to be in Prophet's presence. The annual clean-up weekend preparing Guidance for a Better Life retreat center grounds for a new year was just wrapping up. We gathered together as Del was about to lead us in singing HU. I always enjoy this opportunity as the group expresses to God the love and gratitude in our hearts.

As I sat down I looked around at the beautiful scene in that room and over at my family with a smile on my face, expressing the joy and gratefulness in my heart. I reflected on the gift of being there together. My husband and I attend retreats offered by Prophet Del Hall on a regular basis. This is where we learned about HU, which is also an ancient name for God. In turn we taught it to our three children and sing it at home, but on this day we would all be participating in singing together at the retreat center.

Prophet led the HU song, and our voices followed in unison, sending love to God, wave after wave as individuals and as a group. There was an immediate response from God. His beautiful Light and Love filled the room and flowed beyond. It showered down to all in attendance and created a brightness spanning throughout the space. I could feel the sound reverberating in my heart and being. This living Light and Sound of God, His Voice, seemed to draw out and showcase Divine qualities as I overflowed with joy, gratitude, and love. This beautiful cycle of giving God love and appreciation, and then receiving His Love continued with no perception of time, until Prophet ended by saying, "Thank you."

As the group dispersed I stood outside by the edge of the building holding my three-year-old son. He kept poking his finger at a wooden post in front of us. His face looked puzzled as he continued this direct and deliberate movement. When I asked what he was doing he said, "What is that Mom?" Chuckling and slightly confused by his question I said, "It is wood. It is part of the building." Still displaying a perplexed look he said, "Hmm… wood, yeah. But this isn't a building, it is a light castle." I was taken aback. Everything stood still in that moment. I was amazed my son could see what I knew to be true based on my own experiences and those shared by others over the years at the retreat center.

In that moment we were both seeing through Soul's eyes, not our physical ones. We had just sung HU with open hearts in the presence of God's Prophet tuning in to Spirit, and there was a higher view before us. We were raised up to see it. My son saw clearly. He was seeing truth. He was experiencing that building as what it really is — not an illusion, but God's Light. And it is everywhere. We just need to look through a new lens. At the same time I was seeing him as Soul, maybe for the first time. It was more personal than seeing others as Soul. This was my own child, and it made an impression. Just as quickly he was back to acting like a little boy and talking about other things, but in that window of a moment my view changed.

He is my son, but really he is Soul first. I knew that, but I experienced it and that changed something. My view, perception, and interactions were different. This experience brought out a desire in me to be more aware of demonstrating for my children how I am led by Prophet and love God. They are each a child of God I am blessed to care for in this life. I am privileged to guide, nurture, encourage, and help them find their way. It is not simply my job to "take care of them" in providing food, clothing, shelter, and supervision, but I am entrusted to love and guide them. I am their mother, but first and foremost they are each a child of God on loan to me to raise. Regardless of their age, they are Soul first. These messages sank into me so much deeper that day.

That one small interaction held layers of lasting truth and lessons I still think about today. With that new image of my son, I recognized my goal to be clear and focused, so I may be the best teacher I can for my children. I want to model for them to the best of my ability, and I can when I am led by Spirit. We simply need to accept the Divine help and guidance that is always available to Soul; just like my little one did that morning, seeing our real surroundings through the eyes of Soul. God's Love is everywhere. Prophet wants to show those willing and ready.

Written by Michelle Hibshman

I Held Her in Heaven

We all, as Soul, live many many lifetimes. During our earthy incarnations we develop love connections with other Souls, and often we are blessed to reincarnate with the same Souls to continue our journey together. The following is a beautiful story of a mother-to-be meeting her future daughter in the inner spiritual worlds, before her physical birth.

I have a daughter who is nearly two and a half years old. My pregnancy with her almost seems like a dream now. I can recall snippets, but mostly I remember the wondering and the waiting. A lot of that goes on in nine months. "What will she be like? Will we get along?" As first-time parents my husband and I really had no clue what to expect. While much of this time is fading from memory there is one experience I had while pregnant I will never forget. It has forever changed the way I see my daughter and the way I view our family. Prophet allowed me to meet and hold my daughter, before she was born, in Heaven.

I was five months pregnant while at a retreat at Guidance for a Better Life. This is one of my favorite places to be. As a group we sang HU and focused on sending our love and gratitude to God. In the quietude after singing HU I left my body spiritually as Soul and Prophet took me to Heaven, our true home. Each journey to this sacred place has been different. Each visit has helped me, degree by degree, to understand the tremendous love God has for me personally and for all of His creation.

This time I knelt with Prophet at the edge of God's Ocean. It was night and the water was calm. It was a gift of love from God to see it this way because there is a special beauty to me about the physical ocean at nighttime. I could feel the Presence of God's Love and peace all around me and in me. I savored being in the moment experiencing the quiet stillness, like being held in a loving embrace.

Just being allowed to be here was a most incredible thing, and yet Prophet gave me another personal and sacred blessing. I looked out across the water to see a beautiful being of light emerge from the velvety depths of God's Ocean. This being was in a female form. As the being came closer I saw she was carrying something, and to my surprise it was the Soul that would be my future daughter, Camille. The beautiful being stood in front of me holding this precious Soul in her arms, as one would cradle a cherished baby. Camille was made of God's Light and Sound. The way she moved in this being's arms was the same as in my womb, as though bursting to get out, a literal bundle of joy.

The being of light silently handed Camille to me with care, and I was allowed to hold her for a moment. It did not feel like my daughter and I were meeting for the first time. It was more a reunion of two Souls happy to see each other once again. I loved her and she loved me. How incredible to know the Soul being born into my family was indeed a Soul I had known and loved before. I was speechless. To be here in Heaven was amazing in itself, but I was also being reunited with a Soul that was to be my future daughter. Now I was even more excited and could not wait for her to be born. I could not wait for the moment when she, Soul, would animate her physical body; the moment when she would take her first breath of life in this world, and I could kiss her sweet face.

Then I gave her back to the being of light who returned into God's Ocean. I was filled with wonder and appreciation that God allowed us to meet in this sacred place. Soul, being eternal, is ageless, yet I was allowed to meet her in the form she would be taking in her new physical embodiment, that of my daughter. In this way I could hold her as I was so longing to do. This was a stunning gift from God.

Being allowed to meet my daughter before she was born into this life taught me more about the remarkable love God has for each Soul. I learned that Soul is a child of God whose true home is in Heaven. Our sons and daughters are not randomly selected, but are given to us with purpose by God's loving design. It does not matter if we are born into a family or adopted. Our families are part of a love story that started before this lifetime and will continue into future lives. In His timing God will reconnect us with our loved ones again.

I am so grateful that Camille joined our family and that I can love her again. She is such a delight! I look forward to the day when I can share with her the story of how I held her in Heaven.

Written by Carmen Snodgrass

A Child of God is Born

Sometimes God pulls back a curtain allowing us to experience the spirituality of a situation. The following is a beautiful testimony of witnessing the sacredness of childbirth. It is at this moment that Soul enters the body and a new adventure begins.

How grateful I am for my children, three gifts that God has bestowed upon my wife and I. What were once happy "additions" to the family are now integral parts that I would not want to imagine our lives without. Each of my children's births was a precious and sacred moment, but it was the birth of my eldest child that gave me a glimpse into the divinity that was clothed in each little bundle of joy.

The morning my eldest child was born, I stood in the delivery room experiencing all the nervousness and excitement of a first-time dad-to-be. My mind raced forwards and backwards as the moment crawled nearer and nearer.

Because I was at the front of the bed, ready to offer sips of water and cold washcloths to my wife, I could see everyone else in the room. Several people, including the doctor, head nurse, and various other nurses and assistants popped in and out. Time seemed to slow to a freeze, and I watched, with this sort of detached viewpoint, a panorama of the other people there.

There was what I can only describe as a reverent anticipation bubbling up in the room. Everyone — it seemed like a lot more than the three or four individuals there — seemed riveted on this sacred moment. There was an overwhelming reverence for Soul permeating the air. A spark of God was about to don another body, take Its knocks, learn Its lessons, and continue on Its journey home to the Heart of God. I believe each person there, whether conscious of it or not, was recognizing Soul — the Divine spark about to be housed in a tiny little body — but also which lived in each other and in themselves. Each in his or her own way recognized that the source of this spark of life was God.

While my wife, the doctor, and several nurses prepared for the imminent birth, a young nursing assistant stood in the middle of the room unconsciously rocking back and forth, in a slow cadence to some distant rhythm only she could hear. She hugged herself instinctively, as if rocking an invisible baby in her arms. It was hard to say if she was imagining comforting the baby about to be born or herself. Maybe both.

When my son finally arrived, I moved into position to "catch" him. I witnessed a ball of glowing light so intense and brilliant it became hard to see anything else. I immediately recognized this Soul as someone I had loved dearly before. Watching Soul enter the body was breathtaking. The doctor and nurses helped guide his tiny body into my arms. I was holding him when he took his first breath in this body, before surrendering him to my wife's welcoming embrace. The recognition between mother and son seemed apparent as well.

In my years at Guidance for a Better Life, Del has repeatedly led me to experiences that have shown me there is so much more to us than just our bodies — much more than just the parts we can normally see. I believe I witnessed a glimpse of that in my son as he was being born, a glimpse into the Divine essence of our being, which is born into this world to learn, to love, and to attempt to pick up the trail back to Its eternal Home.

Written by Chris Comfort

I Am Soul

One of the most critical understandings the Prophet helps seekers come to is this: you do not "have" a Soul, rather, you "are" Soul — you "have" a body. At first this is merely a concept, but as you experience it for yourself in ever-greater capacities, it will truly set you free. In many ways this one truth is the gateway to almost boundless spiritual experiences and consciousness.

While participating in a guided spiritual exercise at Guidance for a Better Life I was given an experience that combined with many previous ones to transform a concept I had to a deeper understanding. Often when we are being taught something new it starts as a concept that grows into a reality as we have personal experiences with what we are being shown.

What comes to mind as an example is when I learned how to ride a bike. I remember seeing others riding around the neighborhood balanced on two wheels and thinking it was a most marvelous adventure and that I wanted to be a part of it. I watched and studied how they got up on the bike, immediately began to pedal, then went soaring down the street. No problem. I had experience on the small bike that my father had taught me how to ride by running along and steadying me when needed.

With days of solo time I felt I was ready to move up to the next level. I begged to borrow one of the older boy's bike assuring him that I knew what I was doing, jumped up on it, reached down with my foot to spin the petals but was soon made aware that the bike was too big and my legs were too short. First try, crash. As the skin grew back on my hands my thought was that it must have been an equipment problem so I went searching for a different bike. I then began to notice that the design difference between a boy's bike and a girl's bike would allow me to reach the pedals in spite of my lack of leg length. The potential threat of ridicule of riding a girl's bike was, in my mind, offset by this being an experiment whose outcome was to have the ability to eventually soar like the older boys.

Fortunately, a girl in the neighborhood had such a bike and was kind enough to lend it to me if I promised to make the necessary repairs after I wrecked it; what a pessimist. No problem.

I jumped up on the bike and began to pedal down the street magically on two wheels at a rapid rate of speed tasting my new found freedom of being able to journey to neighborhoods I had never been, to see and do things in one afternoon that I had only dreamed of, expanding horizons before me ... until I hit the parked car. Turning and stopping effectively didn't happen as easily as I thought it would. Second try, crash. Because of the damage to the car's tail light, the neighbor girl's bike, and my bloodied face, my father was now involved. In hindsight it was a blessing that saved me from myself. All the allowance money that I had to my name and all future earnings for quite some time went to providing restitution for the damage I caused.

My parents gave me an appropriately sized bike for my next birthday with my father teaching me how to properly ride a bike in the evenings after he came home from work. Because of his insights, instructional abilities, the faith he had in me, and the experience I had from the previous wrecks, I was soon soaring down the road. The concept of riding a bike had become a reality that grew to levels I would never have imagined. Riding at breakneck speeds through the woods, going on long day trips, jumping off ramps, towing skaters behind with a rope, and eventually evolving to riding dirt bikes and cruising motorcycles. Such joy and freedom were found in the reality of riding a bike.

When my spiritual instruction began at Guidance for a Better Life one of the basic tenets I was taught is that we are Soul. We don't have a Soul but are Soul with a physical body. When going home one day after having attended a weekend spiritual retreat I saw a bumper sticker stating that we are spiritual beings having a physical experience. Seeing it stated in another form allowed me to better understand it. Throughout the years during spiritual exercises, I have been shown by the

Prophet the limitlessness of Soul. I have been taken to spiritual temples, met spiritual masters, and been before the Light of God. Throughout my day I know a communication with the Prophet that is received in my heart, as Soul, which guides me in all aspects of my life. Like learning to ride a bike the concept was growing into a reality.

During the spiritual experience I mentioned in the beginning, the Prophet took us to the Abode of God. We began by singing HU, a love song to God. I soon became aware that I was kneeling on a golden beach facing an ocean of the most beautiful waters that were gently lapping at my knees. I was a light body, Soul, without physical limitations. Up and down the beach were other light bodies kneeling on the sand, some I knew as fellow students, all I knew were guided here by the Prophet.

On the horizon was the Light of God expanding towards us. During previous experiences the light had grown into an intensity that is beyond words that flowed into me cleansing and filling every recess of my being. This time the light was softer as if I was seeing it from beside the source of the light. Imagine what it is like to have a strong light shone on you; it is intense and it is all you can see. Now imagine how it would be to stand by the source of the light; it would be more diffused and illuminate all it was shined on. Coming across the ocean with the light was a sound, a vibration, the music of the Love of God that was expanding into all creation. I was reminded of the words of a great spiritual master: "The Light and Sound was of a wondrous whiteness like falling snow..." This one more experience expanded, deepened my knowingness of truly existing as Soul. Only as Soul could I have known the Light of God, the Love of God, in this form and magnitude. Only as Soul could I have known God's Light and Sound as one of the masters does. God so loves me that He stood me by His side and guided me to a deeper understanding. I am blessed, by His Grace, to have been given this gift. He knew exactly what I needed and when I was ready to more fully know my true self, Soul.

Like my father who wanted to show me how to properly ride a bike and open the possibilities of adventure for me, our Heavenly Father wants us to know that we are Soul, a Divine being that He loves completely. When the truth that we are Soul grows from concept to reality, worlds of awareness are open to us and our spiritual growth is limitless. Accept the Prophet as your teacher and you will experience the joy and freedom of knowing your true self. I AM SOUL, YOU ARE SOUL.

Written by Terry Kisner

Part Four: What It Is Like Living from a Higher View of Life

There is a fundamental principle that relates to spiritual growth and is one of the Spiritual Keys in Prophet Del Hall's book, *Spiritual Keys For a More Abundant Life*. The Key of Spiritual Growth tells us there is always more to learn of God's ways, His truths, and the vast inner Heavenly worlds He created. There is also always more growth and learning in regards to ourselves: understanding our lower self (physical) and our higher self, including the splendors of Soul; how with Soul in charge the higher and lower selves can come into alignment and work in harmony together; and the completeness that can be experienced when the two operate as one. Prophet Del Hall's video "Parable of a Spiritual Journey" compares Soul's journey through Its many incarnations during Its one eternal life as Soul to climbing a vast mountain, the mountain of God. It is a journey that takes place over many physical lifetimes and begins with an individual Soul on a meandering walk through a valley of many winding and intersecting paths, different religions and spiritual beliefs that bring a certain degree of growth but all leading to the base of an enormous mountain. At this point the individual is no longer "wandering" spiritually speaking from religion to religion and is now looking for higher truths than were found in the valley. Soul is beginning to stir and "wake up" spiritually and is wanting something "more." Perhaps It has become more desirous of knowing God and His ways and truth. Or perhaps one doesn't know what they are looking for, specifically, but somehow innately knows there is more. The individual is now a seeker, and thus, begins the long trek up the vast mountain of God where they meet God's Prophet who is there to guide and show the way. As one becomes more and more receptive to the help, a form of God's Love that is offered through His Prophet, the parable tells us how we are led further and further up the mountain by Prophet, the higher views of life we reach and the abundance this brings. Prophet's parable also talks of the precious and sacred relationship we have the opportunity to develop with both God and His Prophet along the way. While I am still very much growing and learning every day, Prophet has guided me high enough up on the mountain of God that I can now see the path he and I have climbed together thus far.

When I first met Del many years ago, I carried a lot of burdens in my spiritual backpack as I journeyed haphazardly in the valley, knowing there was something more to the aimless searching and wandering I did, looking to fill the void of something unknown to me but I knew was missing in my life. My backpack was laden with unhappiness and pain of the heart because of the way I was living. I was living primarily from my lower self back then because I didn't know anything different. I was often unhappy and often felt lost, confused, and lacked stability and purpose in life. I felt sort of hollow inside and not connected to anything as if adrift on the ocean, bobbing like a cork. I felt separate and distant from the God I innately loved. Experiencing life like this also left little room for love, real love. For as long as I can remember I had been looking for love, many times in desperate ways or wrong places. As a child, I craved attention and dreamed of falling in love someday and getting married. As an adult, I yearned for affection and intimacy, never ever feeling I could get enough. No priest or nun in my twelve years of Catholic school or decades of sermons from churchgoing ever spoke about a "higher self" or the Divine nature of Soul. Not one word was uttered of the world of difference there was in the quality of life or joy and abundance one could experience when living from this higher self and the extraordinary view it brings. They simply did not know anything about this. From their view, that degree of happiness, abundance, and joy was something only to be experienced after we die physically and it was beyond their level of knowledge and understanding of God's ways and truths. A higher, more complete knowledge and wisdom of God is entrusted to His Prophets. The role and job of God's Prophet are expansive and highly specialized, requiring lifetimes of preparation and training in the ways and truths of God. God personally handpicks His special Emissaries to Earth, His Prophets. When they are ordained by God to be His Prophet, He gives them the spiritual authority and wisdom to teach His children these higher truths, which are unknown in their totality and purity to priests and clergy.

Thinking back on how life was for me before I became Del's student causes me to shake my head and think — wow. It is a reminder of how much my life has changed and how differently I see things now versus back then. We are so much more than we think. We are not defined by being male or female, a particular race, skin color, religious affiliation, age, or any other physical or social label. We are Soul! Our essential nature is Divine because we were created by God in His image and endowed with Divine qualities.

As Soul we are eternal and are given the gift of time to learn lifetime after lifetime; this is our spiritual journey up the metaphorical mountain of God. We are all on a journey of this kind whether we realize it or not. Our journeys span many incarnations in a grand adventure that will eventually lead us up the mountain, becoming more mature spiritual beings and back home to the Heart of God where we were first created. This homecoming is not the end of the adventure, however, and in many ways it is just the beginning! Once we get to the top of the mountain, Prophet tells us, we will discover there is yet another mountain, for there is always more!

Lifetime after lifetime we incarnate here on planet Earth, which is really an "Earth school," to learn the ways of God and how to give and receive love. At the center of most of the lessons of living we encounter on our journey, is an opportunity to learn about love and become better at giving and receiving love. This is the big picture, the higher and more expansive view of Soul as contrasted to the narrow, lower view I once held years ago. From the view of Soul, as we travel higher up the mountain with Prophet, there is a boundless expanse that begins to come into view. We begin to see from whence we came and have perspective unlike any we have had to this point. As Prophet teaches us God's ways and truths and we live righteously in accordance with them, we grow. We travel further and higher up the mountain with God's Wayshower expertly leading the way. God's Love and Grace through Prophet lift us to a higher and more expansive view and a whole new world of unlimited possibility and love awaits. We begin to see the infinite ways love can be expressed and appreciate all the ways it may come back to us. We begin to think of others more often than ourselves and naturally want to give love for the pure joy of it. The size and packaging of the love that's delivered do not make it more or less significant. Any act, no matter how seemingly small, if motivated by love is special and is profound. Love is love.

My view today is a higher view than the one I had decades ago when I was down in the valley. It is a stunning view of life! It is something I wanted to try to describe to you because until you experience it for yourself, there is just no other way to understand how different life can be. How amazing and beautiful every day can be. How breathtaking watching the Hand of God in the world can be and the awe and reverence one can experience when in the presence of the Holy of Holies, the Almighty God, our Creator. Along the way as Prophet was guiding me up the mountain of God, everything became about my relationship with him, mostly because I had grown to love him so much there wasn't anything I wanted to do without him. I realized that not only could I not have gotten there without all his help, but I also could not go any further without his continued guidance, wayshowing, protection, and love. All life became spiritual. I began to see God's Hand in all areas of my life and realized how much our Heavenly Father loves us, His children. He loves us so completely, so personally that there is nothing He wouldn't do for us if it would bless us. I couldn't see this down in the valley because I had different wants and desires back then that were not in my best interest. I often hid from the truth and did not seek the Kingdom of God nor put God first in my life. When I did though, and aligned myself with God's ways and truths, trying my best to live them, His Grace flowed into my life in countless ways, many I will probably never know. One of these gifts of God's Grace was being led to Del and becoming a student of the current Prophet of God. This singular event was a major turning point on my journey because Prophet met me as a lost seeker on the foothills of God's mountain and began to show me the way home to God, step by step helping me climb higher and higher.

From my view today, I can now see how God provides for all my daily needs and even the unspoken desires deep in my heart only He could know, provided they are in my best interest and do not negatively impact or encroach on another Soul or their free will. I began to see just how responsive the Heavenly Father actually is to the desires and prayers in my heart. I came to want nothing more than to love Him back and serve Him in the perfect and unconditional way He loves me, even if my degree of perfect could only be to my measure. I still want to model His perfect Love. I have respect for all life I did not have before because it is the handwork of our Creator. I experience reverence and sacredness in daily life never before known because I live in the presence of God's Prophet, God's Holy Spirit, and every moment is a moment I can be in communication with my Maker, even if that communication is expressed through listening for His gentle whisperings or inner guidance. I often just want to go to my knees when I pray because of the magnificence, greatness, and reverence I experience in His Presence.

There are times in class at the retreat center when I experience this same reverence in Del's presence when he is teaching. My heart is exponentially more open and receptive to God's Love when I am in Del's physical presence. It is in part because he is a concentrated aspect of God's Holy Spirit and Soul is naturally uplifted and more open to God's Love in a Prophet's presence, if receptive. As God's Prophet, Del brings an extraordinary amount of Light and Sound into the physical world and I feel this as Soul. As I learned to give and receive love in a more pure way, I began to learn more of what I was made of and who I truly was as the Divine Soul God created. Life becomes more abundant when we live in accordance with God's ways, which includes living as our true selves. I found this to be so true. Living life as Soul is a completely different experience from living from the human state of consciousness. I am joyful and happy most of the time. I have a sense of peace and inner stability that endures no matter the outer circumstances of the day. I am anchored in God's Love, Light, and Sound through my relationship with my beloved Prophet, and I never feel alone. With Prophet as my guide and God's eternal teachings to light my way in life, I never feel lost or adrift. They are my inner compass so I can always find my way through any challenge or difficulty.

God's Love, Grace, and spiritual guidance through His Prophet, Del Hall III, has helped me grow from seeing from the condensed, narrow view of the lower self to having the higher view of Soul. God's Grace cleared the foggy mists of illusion I wandered in down in the valley and brought clarity and enlightenment. Having the privilege of being Del's student for over twenty-six years at the time of this writing has brought me this clarity, this extraordinary view of life, and so much more! I found myself, I found happiness, peace, and joy, and I found that which I have hungered for so long — God's pure, deeply satisfying Love. Because God's Love flows through Del in such a pure way, he has been and will continue to be the greatest teacher and my role model of love for all time. He has opened my eyes and my heart to the beauty of true love and the joy of living a life of service and obedience to God, my Heavenly Father.

Written by Lorraine Fortier

Guidance for a Better Life
Our Story

My Father's Journey

God always has a living Prophet on earth to teach His ways and accomplish His will. My father, Del Hall III, is currently God's true Prophet fully raised up and ordained by God Himself. He was not always a

Prophet Del Hall III

Prophet, nor did he even know what a Prophet was, but God had a plan for him like He has for all of His children. Over many years through many life experiences, God had begun to prepare my father for his future assignment, mostly unbeknownst to him. Everything he experienced in his life from the joys to the sadness helped prepare him for his future role as Prophet.

My dad grew up in California and was a decent student but a better athlete. He received an appointment to the United States Naval Academy in Annapolis, Maryland where he later met my mother. They were married two days after he graduated and received his commission as an officer. After a short tour on a Navy ship deployed to Vietnam, he went to flight training school and became a Navy fighter pilot. While attending flight school in Pensacola, Florida he also earned a Master of Science Degree and had the first of his three children, a son. After flight school he was stationed in a fighter squadron on the east coast, where he and my mom began investing in real estate, adding to their family with the birth of two daughters. Following this tour of duty he was assigned as a jet flight instructor in Texas, after which, his time in the Navy was finished. He was a natural pilot and loved his time in the sky, but it was time to move on.

So far in life he had no real concern for, or even thought much about God, religion, or spiritual matters in general. He lived life fully. He raised his family. He traveled. He invested and became an entrepreneur starting and growing highly successful businesses in diverse fields ranging from real estate to aerospace consulting. Years before however, a seed had been planted when God's eternal teachings were introduced to him in his late teens, and while it did not show outwardly, the truth in these teachings spoke to his heart. My dad might not have been giving much thought to God up to this point in his life, but God was definitely thinking about him and the future He had planned for him. Like an acorn destined to become a mighty oak, the seed that lay dormant in his heart would someday be stirred to life. Through all his life experiences, both "good" and "bad," God would be preparing him for his future role as His Prophet.

When God decided it was time, He called my dad to Him. He did this by shutting down the world of financial security my dad had built. Over a period of two years all of his businesses were wound down and dissolved. What seemed like security turned out to be an illusion. Financial success had not provided true security. He now had failed businesses and a failing marriage and was trying to fix things without God's help, principles, or guidance. As painful as this time in his life was, it was yet another step towards the glorious life of service awaiting my father. God was removing him from the world my dad had created and furthering him along his path to his future role as Prophet.

After his marriage ended and his businesses wound down, he started fresh by going out west to give flying lessons near Lake Mead, Nevada. While living in Nevada my dad was reintroduced to the eternal teachings of God he first learned of as a teenager twenty-three years earlier, and though they resonated with him at the time, his priorities were different back then. Now, his serious training could begin. He started having very clear experiences with the Holy Spirit and noticed there was a familiarity with these teachings and experiences. He embraced the long hours of instruction, which often lasted until sunrise, and was receptive to the personal spiritual experiences he was given. This began an intense period of study and desire for spiritual truth that continues to this day. Some of his most profound and meaningful experiences during this time were with past Prophets of old. They came to him spiritually in contemplations and dreams. He learned of their roles in history and how they were raised up and ordained by God directly. He began to realize they were training him but was not clear why. A few times his experiences led him to believe he was in training to be a future Prophet. However, that revelation made no sense to him because he felt he was an imperfect person who made mistakes and had failures. He thought of the past and current Prophets of God as perfected Souls, not imperfect like he felt he was. Why would God choose him for such a role? He did not feel qualified.

Besides being introduced to God's teachings while he was out west, my father was blessed to meet his current wife Lynne. Returning to the East Coast, my father and Lynne moved into a small cabin on land he had acquired before his businesses shut down. This was a major change in his life, but it felt deeply right within him. He began to remember a desire to live like this as a child; from early childhood my dad found clarity and peace in nature. He had forgotten about this until now, but God had not and made this dream a reality. In addition to being their home, these beautiful, three-hundred-plus acres of land in the Blue Ridge Mountains would eventually become the location for the Guidance for a Better Life retreat center. The perfection of my father's experiences from earlier in his life in real estate, providing the land for his next step in life, speak to the perfection of God's plan. One of many many examples I could list.

For many years my dad took wilderness skills courses around the country. He specialized in the study of wild edible and medicinal plants, tracking, and awareness skills, and authored articles for publication. Inspired to help folks feel more comfortable in the outdoors, my dad and Lynne began the Nature Awareness School in 1990. Classes were focused on teaching awareness and the primitive living skills needed to enjoy the woods and survive in them if necessary. An amazing thing happened within those first few years though; students began to experience aspects of God in very personal and dramatic ways. Somewhat like my dad's experience out west, they found that stepping away from their daily routine and the hustle of life, if even for a few days, created space for Spirit to do Its work. Whether they were enjoying the beauty of the Virginia wilderness and tranquility of the school grounds or relaxing by the pond, he found students' hearts opened, and they became more receptive to the Divine Hand that is always reaching out to Its children. More and more the discourse during wilderness classes shifted to the meanings of dreams, personal growth, finding balance in life, and experiences the students were having with the Voice of God in Its many forms. An increase of spiritual retreats was offered to fulfill the demand and over time became the predominant class offerings; the wilderness survival skills classes eventually fading away completely. The name "Nature Awareness School" seemed to be less fitting for what was actually being taught now and in February 2019 my father changed the name of the retreat center to Guidance for a Better Life.

Throughout this time my father's training and spiritual study continued. My father reached mastership and was ordained by God on July 7, 1999 but he was still not yet Prophet, more was required. On October 22, 2012, twenty-five years since his full-time intensive training had begun, God ordained him as His chosen Prophet, and He has continued to raise him up further since. God works through my father in very direct and beneficial ways for his students. Hundreds and hundreds of students over the past thirty years have received God's eternal teachings through my father's instruction and mentoring. They have had personal experiences with the Divine which have transformed and greatly blessed their lives. My father's greatest joy is being used by God as a servant to share God's ways and truths with thirsty Souls and hungry seekers. In addition to mountaintop retreats, my father continues to spread God's ways and teachings that so greatly blessed his life and the lives of his loved ones in many ways.

The book you hold in your hand is but one of more than a dozen titles we have co-authored. These incredible testimonies of God's Love are being shared in print, eBook, audio, YouTube videos and podcasts in hopes of blessing others.

Maybe you are at a turning point in your life and looking for direction. Maybe you have a knowing there is more to life but not sure what that might be or how to find it. Or, maybe you are simply drawn to what you read and hear in our stories. God speaks to our hearts and calls each of us in many different ways. Like my father's journey demonstrates, it doesn't matter where you started or the twists, turns, or seeming dead-ends your life has taken; God wants us to know Him more fully, and for us to know our purpose within His creation. He wants us to experience His Love regardless of our religious path or lack thereof. He always has a living Prophet here on Earth to help us accomplish His desire for us — to show us the way home to Him and to experience more abundance in our life while we are still living here on Earth. God's Prophet today is my father, Del Hall III. You have the opportunity to grow spiritually through God's teachings which Prophet shares. His guidance for a better life is available for you — please accept it.

Written by Del Hall IV

My Son, Del Hall IV

My son, Del Hall IV, joined Guidance for a Better Life as an instructor after fifteen years of in-class training with me, his father. He helped develop the five step "Keys to Spiritual Freedom"

Del Hall IV

study program and facilitates the first two courses in the program: Step One "Tools for Divine Guidance" and Step Two "Understanding Divine Guidance." Del also teaches people about the rich history of dream study and how to better recall their own dreams during the "Dream Study Workshops," which he hosts around the country. He is qualified to step in and facilitate any of my retreats should the need arise.

Del is also Vice President of Marketing and helps with everything required to get the "good news" from Guidance for a Better Life out to hungry seekers: everything from book publishing, blogging, podcasts, and other social media outlets. He is co-author and book cover designer for many of our, thus far, fourteen published books.

My son loves the opportunity to work on creative projects for Guidance for a Better Life. From a very early age he has been an artist and loved creating artwork in multiple mediums. He was accepted into gifted art programs in Virginia Beach and then after high school graduation he attended the School of the Museum of Fine Arts in Boston. He is now a nationally exhibited artist and his paintings of the Light and Sound of God are in over seventy-five public and private collections. One of the greatest joys of the painting process for Del is using his paintings as an opportunity to share with others the inspiration behind them, God's Love and his experiences with the Light and Sound of God, the Holy Spirit, in contemplation and in waking life.

Del lives on the retreat center property in the Blue Ridge Mountains of Virginia with his wife and my three grandchildren whom they homeschool. He loves woodworking, tending to his vegetable garden, pruning his fruit trees, and helping maintain the beautiful three-hundred acres of retreat center property for students to enjoy. There is always something that needs attention on the land and Del is always up to the challenge. He loves to travel and spends his free time enjoying this beautiful country with his family in their RV.

My son has had multiple brain surgeries starting when he was seventeen years old for a recurring brain tumor. He credits God for surviving and thriving all this time when most with his condition do not. He looks to the sunrise every day with gratitude for yet another chance at life. With that chance he desires to help me share the love and teachings of God that have so blessed our lives. I pray to God daily thanking Him for my son's good health.

Written by Prophet Del Hall III

What is the Role of God's Prophet?

An introductory understanding of God's handpicked and Divinely trained Prophet is necessary to fully benefit from reading this book. God ALWAYS has a living Prophet of His choice on Earth. He has a physical body with a limited number of students, but the inner spiritual side of Prophet is limitless. Spiritually he can help countless numbers of Souls all over the world, no matter what religion or path they are on — even if that is no path at all. He teaches the ways of God and shares the Light and Sound of God. He delivers the living Word of God. Prophet can teach you physically as well as through dreams, and he can lift you into the Heavens of God. He offers protection, peace, teachings, guidance, healing, and love.

Each of God's Prophets throughout history has a unique mission. One may only have a few students with the sole intent to keep

God's teachings and truth alive. God may use another to change the course of history. God's Prophets are usually trained by both the current and former Prophets. The Prophet is tested and trained over a very long period of time. The earlier Prophets are physically gone but teach the new Prophet in the inner spiritual worlds. This serves two main purposes: the trainee becomes very adept at spiritual travel and gains wisdom from those in whose shoes he will someday walk. This is vital training because the Prophet is the one who must safely prepare and then take his students into the Heavens and back.

There are many levels of Heaven, also called planes or mansions. Saint Paul once claimed to know a man who went to the third Heaven. Actually it was Paul himself that went, but the pearl is, if there is a third Heaven, it presumes a first and second Heaven also exist. The first Heaven is often referred to as the Astral plane. Even on just that one plane of existence there are over one hundred sub-planes. This Heaven is where most people go after passing, unless they receive training while still here in their physical body. Without a guide who is trained properly in the ways of God a student could misunderstand the intended lesson and become confused as to what is truth. The inner worlds are enormous compared to the physical worlds. They are very real and can be explored safely when guided by God's Prophet.

Part of my mission is to share more of what is spiritually possible for you as a child of God. Few Souls know or understand that God's Prophet can safely guide God's children, while still alive physically, to their Heavenly Home. Taking a child of God into the Heavens is not the job of clergy. Clergy have a responsibility to pass on the teaching of their religion exactly as they were taught, not to add additional concepts or possibilities. If every clergy member taught their own personal belief system no religion could survive for long. Then the beautiful teachings of an earlier Prophet of God would be lost. Clergy can be creative in finding interesting and uplifting ways to share their teachings, but their job is to keep their religion intact.

However, God sends His Prophets to build on the teachings of His past Prophets, to share God's Light and Love, to teach His language, and to guide Souls to their Heavenly Home.

There is ALWAYS MORE when it comes to God's teachings and truth. No one Prophet can teach ALL of God's ways. It may be that the audience of a particular time in history cannot absorb more wisdom. It could be due to a Prophet's limited time to teach and limited time in a physical body on Earth. Ultimately, it is that there is ALWAYS MORE! Each of God's Prophets brings additional teachings and opportunities for ways to draw closer to God, building on the work and teachings of former Prophets. That is one reason why Prophets of the past ask God to send another; to comfort, teach, and continue to help God's children grow into greater abundance. Former Prophets continue to have great love for God's children and want to see them continue to grow in accepting more of God's Love. One never needs to stop loving or accepting help from a past Prophet in order to grow with the help of the current Prophet.

All true Prophets of God work together and help one another to do God's work.

All the testimonies in this book were written by students at the Guidance for a Better Life retreat center. It is here that the nature of God, the Holy Spirit, and the nature of Soul are EXPERIENCED under the guidance of a true living Prophet of God. Guidance for a Better Life is NOT a religion, it is a retreat center. God and His Prophet are NOT disparaging of any religion of love. However, the more a path defines itself with its teachings, dogma, or tenets, the more "walls" it inadvertently creates between the seeker and God. Sometimes it even puts God into a smaller box. God does not fit in any box. Prophet is for all Souls and is purposely not officially aligned with any path, but shows respect to all.

YOU can truly have an ABUNDANT LIFE through a personal and loving relationship with God, the Holy Spirit, and God's ordained Prophet. This is my primary message to you. Having a closer relationship with the Divine requires understanding the "Language of the

Divine." God expresses His Love to us, His children, in many different and sometimes very subtle ways. Often His Love goes unrecognized and unaccepted because His language is not well known. The testimonies in this book have shown you some of the ways in which God expresses His Love. It is my hope that in reading this book, you have begun to learn more of the "Language of the Divine." The stories span from very subtle Divine guidance to profound examples of experiencing God up close and very personal. After reading this book I hope you now know your relationship with God has the potential to be more profound, more personal, and more loving than any organized religion on Earth currently teaches.

If you wish to develop a relationship with God's Prophet, seek the inner side of Prophet, for he is spiritually already with you. Few are able to meet the current physical incarnation and most people do not need to meet Prophet physically. Gently sing HU for a few minutes and then sing "Prophet" with love in your heart and he will respond. It may take time to recognize his presence, but it will come. The Light and Love that flows through him is the same that has flowed through all of God's true Prophets.

A more abundant life awaits you,

Prophet Del Hall III

HU — An Ancient Name For God

HU is an ancient name for God that can be sung quietly or aloud in prayer. HU has existed since the beginning of time in one form or another and is available to all regardless of religion. It is a pure way to express your love to God and give thanks for your blessings.

Singing HU (HUUUUUU pronounced "hue") serves as a tuning fork with Spirit that brings you into greater harmony with the Divine. We recommend singing HU a few minutes each day. This can bring love, joy, peace, and clarity, or help you rise to a higher view of a situation when upset or fearful.

Articles of Faith

Written by Prophet Del Hall III

1. We believe in one true God that is still living and active in our lives. He is knowable and wants a relationship with each of His children. He is the same God Jesus called FATHER, and is known by many names, including Heavenly Father. God wants a loving personal relationship with each of us, NOT one based upon fear or guilt.

2. The Holy Spirit is God's expression in all the worlds. It is in two parts, the Light and the Sound. It is through His Holy Spirit God communicates and delivers all His gifts: peace, clarity, love, joy, healings, correction, guidance, wisdom, comfort, truth, dreams, new revelations, and more.

3. God always has a chosen living Prophet to teach His ways, speak His living word, lift up Souls, and bring us closer to God. God's living Prophet is a concentrated aspect of the Holy Spirit, the Light and Sound, and is raised up

and ordained by God directly. His Prophet is empowered and authorized to share God's Light and Sound and to correct misunderstandings of His ways. There are two aspects of God's Prophet, an inner spiritual and outer physical Prophet. The inner Prophet can teach us through dreams, intuition, spiritual travel, inner communication, and his presence. The outer Prophet also teaches through his discourses, written word, and his presence. Prophet is always with us spiritually on the inner. Prophet points to and glorifies the Father.

4. God so loves the world and His children He has always had a long unbroken line of His chosen Prophets. They existed before Jesus and after Jesus. Jesus was God's Prophet and His actual SON. God's chosen Prophets are considered to be in the "role of God's Son," though NOT literally His Son. Only Jesus was literally His son. Prophets were sometimes called Paraclete. The Bible uses the word Comforter, but the original Greek word was Paraclete, which is more accurate. Paraclete implied an actual physical person who helps,

counsels, encourages, advocates, comforts, and sets free.

5. Our real and eternal self is called Soul. We are Soul; we do NOT "have" a Soul. As Soul we are literally an individualized piece of God's Holy Spirit, thereby Divine in nature. We are made of God's Light and Sound, which is actually God's Love. As an individual and uniquely experienced Soul you have free will, intelligence, imagination, opinions, clear and continuous access to Divine guidance, and immortality. As Soul we have an innate and profound spiritual growth potential. Soul has the ability to travel the Heavens spiritually with Prophet to gain truth and wisdom, and grow in love. Soul exists because God loves It.

6. We believe Soul equals Soul, in that God loves all Souls equally and each Soul has the same innate qualities and potential. Soul is neither male nor female, any particular race, nationality, or age. All Souls are children of God.

7. We believe in one eternal life as Soul. However, we believe Soul needs to incarnate

many times into a physical body to learn and grow spiritually mature. Soul's journey home to God encompasses many lifetimes. A loving God does not expect His children to learn His ways in a single lifetime.

8. We believe Soul incarnates on Earth to grow in the ability to give and receive love.

9. We believe God is more interested in two Souls experiencing love for one another than in their sexual preference.

10. It is God's will that a negative power exists to help Soul grow spiritually through challenges and hardships, thereby strengthening and maturing Soul. We are never given a challenge greater than our ability to find a solution. Soul has the ability to rise above any obstacles with God's help.

11. We study the Bible as an authentic teaching tool of God's ways, in addition to books and discourses authored by a Prophet chosen by God. We know the original Biblical writings have been altered in some cases by incorrect translations and political interference throughout the ages. God loves each of us

regardless of our errors. We do not believe in God's eternal abandonment or damnation. He would never turn His back to us for eternity.

12. Karma is the way in which the Divine accounts for our actions, words, thoughts, and attitudes. One can create positive or negative karma. Karma is a blessing used to teach us responsibility. We do not have to earn God's Love, He loves us unconditionally.

13. We do not believe that a child is born in sin, though the child may have karma from a former life. Karma, God's accounting system, explains our birth circumstances better than the concept of sin.

14. We believe that a living Prophet, including Jesus, can remove karma and sin when necessary to help us get started or to grow on the path to God. However, it is primarily our responsibility to live and grow in the ways of God, thereby not creating negative karma and sin.

15. There are four commandments of God in which we abide: First — Love God with all your heart, mind and Soul; Second — Love

your neighbor as yourself. We believe the Third is, "Seek ye first the Kingdom of God, and His righteousness." We believe this means that it is primarily our responsibility to draw close to God, learn His ways, and strive to live the way God would like us to live. God's Prophets are sent to show His ways. We believe our purpose, the Fourth Commandment, is to become spiritually mature to be used by God to bless His children. Becoming a co-worker with God is our primary purpose in life and the most rewarding attainment of Soul.

16. We believe all Souls upon translation, death of the physical body, go to the higher worlds, called Heavens, Planes, or Mansions, regardless of their beliefs. The way they live life on Earth and the effort made to draw close to God impacts the area of Heaven they are to be sent. Those who draw close to a Prophet of God receive special care. We know of twelve distinct Heavens, not one. The primary abode of the Heavenly Father is in the twelfth Heaven, known as the "Ocean of Love and Mercy." We can visit God while we still

live on Earth, but only if taken by His chosen Prophet and only as Soul, not in a physical body.

17. We believe prayer is communication with God and is an extreme privilege. God hears every prayer from the heart whether or not we recognize a response. Singing an ancient name of God, HU, is our foundational prayer. It expresses love and gratitude to God and is unencumbered by words. Singing HU has the potential to raise us up in consciousness making us more receptive to God's Love, Light, and guiding Hand. After praying it is best to spend time listening to God. Prayer should never be rote or routine. We desire to trust God and surrender to His will rather than our own will.

18. We believe it is our responsibility to stay spiritually nourished. When Soul is nourished and fortified It becomes activated and we are more receptive and have clearer communication with the Divine. We believe when Jesus said "give us this day our daily bread," he meant daily spiritual nourishment, not physical bread. This can be done by

singing HU, reading scripture, praying, dream study, demonstrating gratitude for our blessings, being in a living Prophet's physical presence, or in his inner presence, or listening to his words.

19. We believe TRUTH has the power to improve every area of our lives, but only if understood, accepted, and integrated into our lives.

20. We believe God and His Prophet guide us in our sleeping dreams and awake dreams as a gift of love. God's Prophet teaches how to understand both types of dreams. All areas of our lives may be blessed by the wisdom God offers each of us directly in dreams.

21. Gratitude is extremely important on our path of love. It is literally the secret of love. Developing an attitude of gratitude is necessary to becoming spiritually mature. Recognizing and being grateful for the blessings of God in our lives is vital to building a loving and trusting relationship with God and His chosen Prophet. A relationship

with God's Prophet is THE KEY to everything good and a life more abundant.

22. We believe in being good stewards of our blessings. We recognize them as gifts of love from God and make the effort to have remembrance. Remembering our blessings helps to keep our heart open to God and builds trust in God's Love for us.

23. We believe in giving others the freedom to make their own choices and live their lives as they wish. We expect the same in return.

24. We believe the Love and Blessings of God and His Prophet are available to all who are receptive. If one desires guidance and help from Prophet, ask from the heart and sing "Prophet." He will respond. One does not need to meet Prophet physically to receive help. To be taught by Prophet it is best to attend a retreat with him in the physical. However, much can be gained by reading or listening to his teachings.

25. We have a responsibility to do our part and let God and His Prophet do their part. This responsibility brings freedom. Our goal is

to remain spiritually nourished, live in balance and harmony, and serve God as a co-worker. Anything is possible with God if we do our part. We pray to use our God-given free will in a way that our actions, thoughts, words, and attitudes testify and bear witness to the Glory and Love of God.

26. We believe there is always more to learn and grow in God's ways and truth. One cannot remain the same spiritually. One must make the effort to move forward or risk falling backward. To grow in consciousness requires change. Spiritual wisdom gained during our earthly incarnations can be taken to the other worlds when we translate, and into future lifetimes, unlike our physical possessions.

Contact Information

Guidance for a Better Life is a worldwide mentoring program provided by Prophet Del Hall III and his son Del Hall IV. Personal one-on-one mentoring at our retreat center is our premier offering and the most direct and effective way to grow spiritually. Spiritual tools, guided exercises, and in-depth discourses on the eternal teachings of God are provided to help one become more aware of and receptive to His Holy Spirit and the abundance that awaits. With this personally-tailored guidance one begins to more fully recognize God's Love daily in their lives, both the dramatic and the very subtle. Over time our mentoring reduces fear, worry, anxiety, lack of purpose, feelings of unworthiness, guilt, and confusion; replacing those negative aspects of life with an abundance of peace, clarity, joy, wisdom, love, and self-respect leading to a more personal relationship with God, more than most know is possible. We also offer our dozen books, YouTube videos, and podcast.

Guidance for a Better Life
P.O. Box 219
Lyndhurst, Virginia 22952
(540) 377-6068
contact@guidanceforabetterlife.com
www.guidanceforabetterlife.com

"A Growing Testament to the Power of God's Love One Profound Book at a Time."

If you could only read one of Prophet Del Hall's books this is the one. It is full of Keys to unlock the treasures of Heaven and bring more of God's Love into your life.

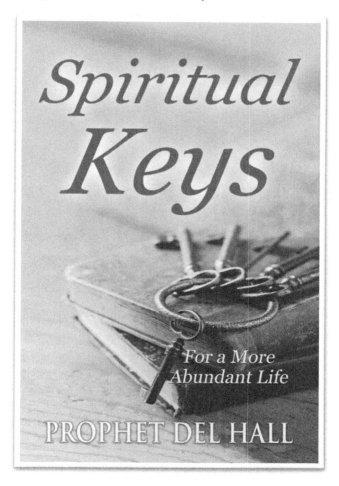

SPECIALIZED TOPICS

Whether you wish to reconnect with a loved one who has passed, understand how you too can experience God's Light, improve your marriage, or learn how to understand your dreams, these incredible books have you covered.

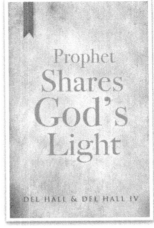

TESTIMONIES OF GOD'S LOVE SERIES

God expresses His Love every day in many different and sometimes subtle ways. Often this love goes unrecognized because the ways in which God communicates are not well known. Each of the books in this series contains fifty true stories that will help you learn to better recognize the Love of God in your life.

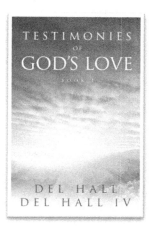 

 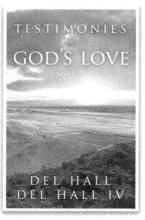

JOURNEY TO A TRUE SELF-IMAGE SERIES

This series includes intimate and unique stories that many readers will be able to personally identify with, enjoy, and learn from. They will help the reader transcend the false images people often carry about themselves — first and foremost that they are only their physical mind and body. The authors share their journeys of recognizing and coming to more fully accept their true self-image, that of Soul — an eternal child of God.

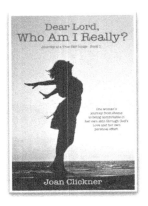

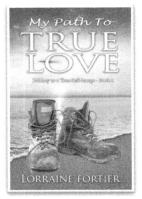

Made in the USA
Middletown, DE
23 June 2023

33290221R00099